Just CHRISTMAS

MARKS &
SPENCER

PLEASE NOTE that the cup and spoon measurements used in this book are metric. A conversion chart appears on page 126.

This edition first published in 2007 by ACP Publishing Pty Limited. Exclusively for Marks and Spencer p.l.c.

www.marksandspencer.com

Copyright ACP Publishing Pty Limited 2007

ISBN: 1-90377707-0

Printed and bound in China

contents

STARTERS & NIBBLES   4

MAIN COURSES   12

VEGETABLES   52

LEFTOVERS   76

COLD DESSERTS   88

CAKES & PUDDINGS   102

CONVERSION CHARTS   126

INDEX   127

STARTERS & NIBBLES

SLOW-COOKED SPICY HERBED PRAWNS

PREPARATION TIME 20 MINUTES * COOKING TIME
30 MINUTES (PLUS REFRIGERATION TIME) * SERVES 8

2kg uncooked medium
king prawns
4 cloves garlic, crushed
2 fresh long red chillies,
chopped coarsely
¾ cup (180ml) olive oil
½ cup (125ml) lemon juice
1 teaspoon sweet paprika
½ cup loosely packed fresh
flat-leaf parsley leaves
½ cup loosely packed fresh
coriander leaves
¼ cup coarsely chopped
fresh chives

1 Preheat oven to slow.
2 Shell and devein prawns, leaving tails intact.
3 Combine garlic, chilli, oil, juice and paprika in shallow
3-litre (12-cup) baking dish, add prawns; toss prawns gently to
coat in mixture. Cook, covered, in slow oven about 30 minutes
or until prawns are just cooked through; stirring once halfway
through cooking time. Cover; refrigerate 2 hours.
4 Serve prawns tossed with herbs.

4

slow-cooked
spicy herbed prawns

SMOKED SALMON & DILLED SOUR CREAM CREPE CAKES

PREPARATION TIME 30 MINUTES (PLUS STANDING TIME) * COOKING TIME 30 MINUTES (PLUS REFRIGERATION TIME) * MAKES 16

½ cup (75g) plain flour
2 eggs
2 teaspoons vegetable oil
1 cup (250ml) milk
2 tablespoons drained capers, rinsed, chopped coarsely
2 tablespoons finely chopped fresh dill
1 tablespoon grated lemon rind
2 teaspoons lemon juice
1 clove garlic, crushed
1 cup (240g) sour cream
500g sliced smoked salmon

1 Line base and side of deep 20cm-round cake tin with clingfilm.

2 Place flour in medium bowl. Make well in centre; gradually whisk in combined eggs, oil and milk. Strain into large jug; stand 30 minutes.

3 Heat oiled 19cm frying pan; pour ¼ cup of the batter into pan, tilting pan to coat base. Cook over low heat, loosening around edge with spatula until browned lightly. Turn; brown other side. Remove from pan; repeat with remaining batter to make a total of five crepes.

4 Combine capers, dill, rind, juice, garlic and sour cream in small bowl. Place a crepe in prepared tin; spread with ½ cup of sour cream mixture, cover with a quarter of the fish. Continue layering with remaining crepes, sour cream mixture and fish, finishing with a crepe. Cover; refrigerate overnight.

5 Gently turn cake onto chopping board; discard clingfilm. Using sharp knife, carefully trim cake into a square; discard trimmings. Cut into 4cm squares; top squares with sour cream and dill, if desired.

pan-fried asparagus
with parmesan

PAN-FRIED ASPARAGUS WITH PARMESAN

PREPARATION TIME 5 MINUTES
* COOKING TIME 5 MINUTES

1 tablespoon olive oil
400g asparagus, trimmed
½ cup (40g) flaked parmesan cheese
½ teaspoon cracked black pepper

1 Heat oil in large frying pan; cook asparagus, in batches, until just tender.
2 Serve asparagus sprinkled with cheese and cracked pepper.

SQUASH & SPINACH FRITTATA

900g squash, sliced thinly
2 cloves garlic, crushed
1 tablespoon olive oil
6 eggs
½ cup (125ml) cream
40g baby spinach leaves
¼ cup (20g) coarsely grated parmesan cheese

PREPARATION TIME 20 MINUTES (PLUS REFRIGERATION TIME) * COOKING TIME 45 MINUTES

1 Preheat oven to moderately hot.
2 Place squash, in single layer, on baking trays; brush with combined garlic and oil. Roast, uncovered, in moderately hot oven until tender.
3 Meanwhile, oil deep 20cm-square cake tin; line base and sides with baking parchment.
4 Whisk eggs with cream in medium jug. Layer half of the squash in prepared tin; pour half of the egg mixture over squash. Top with spinach and remaining squash then pour in remaining egg mixture; sprinkle with cheese.
5 Bake, uncovered, in moderately hot oven about 25 minutes or until firm. Stand 5 minutes before cutting into triangles.

ROASTED VEGETABLE & GOAT'S CHEESE TERRINE

PREPARATION TIME 30 MINUTES *
COOKING TIME 25 MINUTES (PLUS
REFRIGERATION TIME) * SERVES 8

2 large red peppers (700g)
2 large aubergines (1kg),
sliced thinly lengthways
2 medium green courgettes
(240g), sliced thinly
lengthways
150g soft goat's cheese
¼ cup (60ml) cream
1 tablespoon lemon juice
½ cup loosely packed fresh
basil leaves
100g mixed salad leaves

BASIL OIL
½ cup (125ml) extra virgin
olive oil
½ cup loosely packed fresh
basil leaves
10g baby spinach leaves
1 tablespoon finely grated
lemon rind

1 Line 1.5-litre (6-cup) terrine dish with clingfilm.
2 Quarter peppers; discard seeds and membranes. Roast under grill or in very hot oven, skin-side up, until skin blisters and blackens. Cover pepper pieces in plastic or paper 5 minutes; peel away skin.
3 Cook aubergines and courgettes in lightly oiled large frying pan, in batches, until browned both sides.
4 Combine cheese, cream and lemon juice in small bowl.
5 Line base and sides of prepared dish with two-thirds of the aubergine, draping aubergine over all sides of dish. Place half of the pepper over base of dish; spread cheese mixture over pepper then top with basil, courgettes, remaining pepper and remaining aubergine. Fold overhanging aubergine at short sides over terrine then fold remaining aubergine over long sides to completely enclose terrine. Cover; refrigerate 30 minutes.
6 Meanwhile, make basil oil.
7 Cut terrine into eight slices. Serve on salad leaves, drizzle with basil oil.

BASIL OIL Blend or process ingredients until smooth. Strain through small muslin-lined strainer into small jug.

MAIN COURSES

Perfect roasts

Roasts are a relatively simple affair, but a few shared tips and tricks will guarantee lip-smacking results.

* Remove any silver sinew from beef fillet to prevent shrinkage and toughening
* Select a baking dish large enough to fit the roast; make sure the meat does not extend over the sides.
* A rack in a baking dish helps good circulation of heat around the meat.
* The meat should have reached room temperature before cooking.
* When tying a roast, wet the kitchen string first. As the string dries (from the heat of the oven) it will shrink, holding the meat firm.
* Before heating the oven, check that the oven racks are in position.
* Meat can be cooked in an oven bag to prevent spatter and retain moisture; however, roasting times may need to be reduced. Follow the instructions on oven bag packaging.
* Very large cuts of meat will need to be turned halfway through roasting.
* The best way to tell if a roast is done is to use a meat thermometer. Insert the thermometer into the thickest part of the joint. Be careful not to touch any bone as this will give you an inaccurate reading. The reading should be 60°C for rare, 70°C for medium and 75°C for well-done.
* Rest the roast, covered in foil, for 10 to 15 minutes before carving, so that the juices 'settle'.
* Carve meat across the grain to ensure tenderness. While carving, hold meat with tongs rather than a fork to prevent juice loss. The best type of knife to use for carving is one with a straight edge, rather than a serrated edge.
* Before roasting a chicken or a turkey, wash it well in cold water, especially inside the cavity. Pat dry inside and out with paper towelling.
* Do not freeze an uncooked, stuffed chicken or turkey. Bird and stuffing can be frozen separately, then thawed before filling with stuffing.
* To test if roast is cooked, prick the thigh flesh where it meets the body with a metal skewer; if the juice that runs out is clear, it's cooked.
* Fill chicken or turkey cavity loosely with stuffing just before roasting; it will swell during cooking. Secure chicken cavity closed with toothpicks or small skewers. Any leftover stuffing can be moistened with a little stock and cooked in lightly oiled mini muffin tins, or formed into a roll and wrapped in lightly oiled aluminium foil. Bake the extra stuffing with the roast for the last 20 minutes of cooking time.
* Tuck wing tips under the body of chicken; tie legs together with string to help bird keep its shape during roasting.
* Baste a roast chicken or turkey only occasionally – frequent basting will result in a pale coloured bird.
* If using a frozen turkey, allow up to three days to thaw in refrigerator.
* To thaw turkey, cut a small corner off the bag in which it is frozen, place turkey in dish. Stand turkey on slight angle so liquid will drain out of the bag as bird defrosts. Discard the liquid from the dish as it accumulates.
* If keeping a cooked chicken overnight, remove any stuffing from the cavity and refrigerate separately.

traditional turkey
& forcemeat stuffing

TRADITIONAL TURKEY
WITH FORCEMEAT STUFFING

We've used pork and chicken in our forcemeat stuffing, however, you can use your favourite mixture of fish, poultry, meat, vegetables or fruit with breadcrumbs and various seasonings.

4.5kg turkey
1 cup (250ml) water
80g butter, melted
¼ cup (35g) plain flour
3 cups (750ml) chicken stock
½ cup (125ml) dry white wine

FORCEMEAT STUFFING
40g butter
3 medium brown onions
(450g), chopped finely
2 bacon rashers (140g), rind
removed, chopped coarsely
1 cup (70g) stale breadcrumbs
2 tablespoons finely chopped
fresh tarragon
½ cup coarsely chopped fresh
flat-leaf parsley
½ cup (75g) coarsely chopped
roasted pistachios
250g pork mince
250g chicken mince

PREPARATION TIME 40 MINUTES * COOKING TIME
3 HOURS 10 MINUTES (PLUS STANDING TIME) *
SERVES 8-12 (DEPENDING ON YOUR MENU)

1 Make forcemeat stuffing.
2 Preheat oven to moderate.
3 Discard neck from turkey. Rinse turkey under cold water; pat dry inside and out with absorbent paper. Fill neck cavity loosely with stuffing; secure skin over opening with toothpicks. Fill large cavity loosely with stuffing; tie legs together with kitchen string.
4 Place turkey on oiled wire rack in large shallow flameproof baking dish; pour the water into dish. Brush turkey all over with half of the butter; cover dish tightly with two layers of greased foil. Roast in moderate oven 2 hours. Uncover turkey; brush with remaining butter. Roast, uncovered, in moderate oven about 45 minutes or until browned all over and cooked through. Remove turkey from dish, cover turkey; stand for 20 minutes.
5 Pour juice from dish into large jug; skim 1 tablespoon of the fat from juice, return to same dish. Skim and discard remaining fat from juice. Add flour to dish; cook, stirring, until mixture bubbles and is well browned. Gradually stir in stock, wine and remaining juice; bring to a boil, stirring, until gravy boils and thickens. Strain gravy into same jug; serve turkey with gravy.

FORCEMEAT STUFFING Melt butter in medium frying pan; cook onion and bacon, stirring, until onion softens. Using hand, combine onion mixture in large bowl with remaining ingredients.

TIP To test if turkey is cooked, insert a skewer sideways into the thickest part of the thigh then remove and press flesh to release the juices. If the juice runs clear, the turkey is cooked. Alternatively, insert a meat thermometer into the thickest part of the thigh, without touching bone; it should reach 90°C.

Pictured on page 13.

GARLIC ROASTED DUCK

A duck wing portion consists of the wing and part of the breast.

2 tablespoons fish sauce
4 cloves garlic, crushed
1 cup (250ml) red wine vinegar
1 large brown onion (200g), coarsely chopped
2 teaspoons juniper berries, bruised
2 teaspoons fennel seeds
4 duck wing portions (1.5kg)
2 tablespoons plain yogurt

PREPARATION TIME 30 MINUTES *
COOKING TIME 50 MINUTES * SERVES 4

1 Combine fish sauce, garlic, vinegar, onion, berries and seeds in medium bowl. Place duck in single layer in shallow dish; pour over vinegar mixture. Cover dish; refrigerate for 3 hours or overnight.

2 Preheat oven to moderate. Remove duck from marinade; reserve marinade.

3 Place duck, skin-side up, on wire rack over baking dish; bake, uncovered, in moderate oven about 45 minutes or until tender.

4 Place reserved marinade in small saucepan; simmer, uncovered, about 5 minutes or until slightly thickened, strain. Stir yogurt into sauce; serve with duck.

TURKEY WITH
LEMON PARSLEY STUFFING

The turkey and the stuffing can be prepared several hours ahead. Stuff turkey just before roasting.

4.5kg turkey
50g butter, melted
1 cup (250ml) water

LEMON PARSLEY STUFFING
125g butter
2 (200g) trimmed celery stalks, chopped finely
8 green onions (green shallots), chopped finely
2 cloves garlic, crushed
6 cups (420g) coarse fresh, white breadcrumbs
1 cup coarsely chopped fresh flat-leaf parsley
1 tablespoon finely grated lemon rind
salt and freshly ground black pepper
1 egg, beaten lightly

GRAVY
¼ cup (35g) plain flour
3 cups (750ml) reduced-salt chicken stock
1 tablespoon redcurrant jelly
2 teaspoons finely chopped fresh mint

PREPARATION TIME 40 MINUTES * COOKING TIME
3 HOURS 20 MINUTES (PLUS STANDING TIME) * SERVES 8

1   Preheat oven to moderate (180°C/160°C fan-forced).
2   Discard neck from turkey. Rinse turkey under cold water; pat dry inside and out with absorbent paper. Fill neck cavity loosely with lemon parsley stuffing; secure skin over opening with toothpicks. Fill large cavity loosely with lemon parsley stuffing; reserve remaining stuffing. Tie legs together with kitchen string; tuck wings under.
3   Place turkey on oiled wire rack in a large flameproof baking dish. Brush turkey all over with half the butter. Rub a little salt into skin. Pour the water into the dish. Cover dish tightly with greased foil; roast in moderate oven for 2 hours. Uncover turkey; brush with remaining butter. Roast, uncovered, in a moderate oven for a further 1 hour or until browned all over and cooked through, brushing with pan juices every 20 minutes. (To test if turkey is cooked, insert a skewer into the thigh; if juices are clear, it is ready.) Remove turkey from dish, cover turkey; stand for 20 minutes while preparing gravy and finishing vegetables.
4   Increase oven temperature to very hot (240°C/220°C fan-forced). Lightly oil 12 mini-muffin tins. Place 1 tablespoon of reserved lemon parsley stuffing in each tin. Bake in very hot oven for 10 minutes or until they are browned and crisp.
5   Serve turkey with gravy and seasonal vegetables.

LEMON PARSLEY STUFFING   Melt the butter in a large frying pan; cook celery, stirring, until softened. Add onion and garlic, cook, stirring, until fragrant. Combine onion mixture in a large bowl with remaining ingredients.

GRAVY   Pour turkey pan juices from dish into a medium jug; reserve 2 tablespoons of fat from the top; discard remaining fat on surface of juices. Heat the fat in same baking dish, add flour; cook, stirring, until mixture is well browned. Gradually stir in reserved pan juices and stock; bring to the boil. Simmer, stirring, until gravy thickens slightly. Stir in jelly and mint. Season to taste with salt and pepper. Strain gravy into a jug.

SLOW-ROASTED TURKEY WITH SAUSAGEMEAT STUFFING & PORT GRAVY

PREPARATION TIME 30 MINUTES *
COOKING TIME 6 HOURS * SERVES 8

4kg turkey
¼ cup (60ml) chicken stock
½ cup (125ml) port
2 tablespoons brown sugar
2 tablespoons vegetable oil
2 tablespoons plain flour

SAUSAGEMEAT STUFFING
2 tablespoons vegetable oil
2 medium brown onions (300g), sliced
500g sausagemeat
4 cups (280g) stale breadcrumbs
2 tablespoons chopped fresh sage
½ cup (60g) chopped walnuts

1 Preheat oven to low. Discard neck and giblets from turkey. Rinse turkey under cold water; pat dry inside and out, tuck wings under body. Spoon stuffing loosely into cavity. Tie legs together with kitchen string.

2 Place turkey into oiled flameproof baking dish; pour stock and half of the port into dish. Cover baking dish tightly with greased foil (if thin, use two layers); bake in low oven for 5½ hours. Remove foil, brush turkey with combined remaining port and sugar. Increase temperature to moderate; bake, uncovered, 30 minutes or until browned.

3 Remove turkey from dish; cover with foil to keep warm. Strain juices from dish into jug; remove fat from juices. You will need 3 cups (750ml) pan juices. Heat oil in same baking dish, stir in flour; stir over heat until well browned. Remove from heat, gradually stir in reserved pan juices; stir over heat until gravy boils and thickens, strain.

4 Serve turkey with gravy.

SAUSAGEMEAT STUFFING Heat oil in large frying pan, add onion; cook, stirring, until browned, cool. Transfer onion to medium bowl; stir in remaining ingredients.

BONED TURKEY BREAST
WITH COUSCOUS STUFFING

Order a 4.5kg fresh boned turkey breast from your butcher for this recipe.

½ cup (80g) sultanas
½ cup (125ml) lemon juice
4.5kg boned turkey breast
1 cup (250ml) chicken stock
¼ cup (60ml) olive oil
1 cup (200g) couscous
¼ cup (40g) toasted green pumpkinseeds
¼ cup (35g) toasted slivered almonds
¼ cup (35g) toasted pecans, chopped coarsely
¼ cup coarsely chopped fresh flat-leaf parsley
¼ cup coarsely chopped fresh coriander
2 eggs, beaten lightly
1 cup (250ml) water
½ cup (125ml) dry white wine
⅓ cup (50g) plain flour
2 cups (500ml) chicken stock, extra
3 cups (750ml) water, extra

PAPRIKA RUB
1 teaspoon fennel seeds
1 teaspoon sweet paprika
½ teaspoon ground ginger
2 teaspoons salt
2 cloves garlic, quartered
2 tablespoons olive oil

PREPARATION TIME 1 HOUR * COOKING TIME 2 HOURS * SERVES 8–12 (DEPENDING ON YOUR MENU)

1 Soak sultanas in small bowl in half of the juice. Make paprika rub.

2 Preheat oven to moderate.

3 Place turkey flat on board, skin-side down; cover with cling-film. Using rolling pin or meat mallet, flatten turkey meat to an even thickness all over.

4 Combine stock, oil and remaining juice in medium saucepan; bring to a boil. Remove from heat; stir in couscous. Cover; stand about 5 minutes or until liquid is absorbed, fluffing with fork occasionally. Transfer couscous mixture to large bowl; stir in sultana mixture, pumpkinseeds, nuts, herbs and egg.

5 With pointed end of turkey breast facing away from you, place couscous stuffing horizontally along centre of turkey meat. Bring the pointed end of breast over stuffing, securing to the neck skin flap with toothpicks. Working from the centre out, continue securing sides of turkey together with toothpicks (you will have a rectangular roll of turkey in front of you). Tie securely with kitchen string at 4cm intervals.

6 Place turkey roll on oiled wire rack in large shallow flame-proof baking dish; add the water and wine to dish. Rub turkey roll with paprika rub; cover dish tightly with two layers of greased foil. Roast in moderate oven 1 hour. Uncover; roast in moderate oven about 45 minutes or until turkey roll is cooked though. Transfer turkey roll to large serving platter; cover to keep warm.

7 Place dish with juice over heat, add flour; cook, stirring, until mixture bubbles and is well browned. Gradually stir in the extra stock and the extra water; bring to a boil. Reduce heat; simmer, stirring, until gravy boils and thickens. Strain gravy into large jug; serve with turkey.

PAPRIKA RUB Using mortar and pestle, crush ingredients until smooth.

boned turkey breast
with couscous stuffing

POMEGRANATE-GLAZED TURKEY WITH CORNBREAD STUFFING

The cornbread stuffing can be made a day ahead.

4kg turkey
20g butter
6 shallots (150g)
1 large apple (200g), cut into 6 wedges
1 tablespoon fresh sage leaves
20 black peppercorns
2 cups (500ml) water
1 cup (250ml) chicken stock
½ cup (125ml) brandy
50g butter, melted
½ cup (125ml) pomegranate molasses
2 tablespoons plain flour

MACERATED FRUIT
¼ cup (35g) coarsely chopped dried apricots
¼ cup (35g) currants
⅓ cup (80ml) brandy

CORNBREAD STUFFING
350g chorizo, chopped finely
1 medium brown onion (150g), chopped coarsely
2 shallots (50g), chopped coarsely
1 large apple (200g), chopped coarsely
1 tablespoon fresh sage leaves, torn
2 cups (500ml) apple juice
3½ cups (340g) coarsely chopped stale cornbread
⅔ cup (180g) macerated fruit

PREPARATION TIME 1 HOUR 30 MINUTES • COOKING TIME 3 HOURS 30 MINUTES (PLUS COOLING AND STANDING TIME) • SERVES 8-12 (DEPENDING ON YOUR MENU)

1 Two days before, make macerated fruit.
2 On the day of roasting the turkey, preheat oven to moderate.
3 Discard neck from turkey. Rinse turkey under cold water; pat dry inside and out with absorbent paper.
4 Heat butter in large saucepan; cook whole shallots and apple, stirring, until browned lightly. Cool 10 minutes; stir in sage and peppercorns. Tuck wings under turkey; fill large cavity loosely with stuffing; tie legs together with kitchen string.
5 Place turkey on oiled wire rack in large shallow flameproof baking dish; pour the water, stock and brandy into dish. Brush all over with melted butter; cover dish tightly with two layers of greased foil. Roast in moderate oven 2 hours 10 minutes.
6 Meanwhile, make cornbread stuffing.
7 Uncover turkey; brush with half of the molasses. Roast, uncovered, in moderate oven about 20 minutes or until browned all over and cooked through, brushing frequently with remaining molasses. Remove from dish, cover; stand 20 minutes.
8 Pour juice from dish into large jug; skim 1 tablespoon of the fat from juice, return to same dish. Skim and discard remaining fat from juice. Add flour to dish; cook, stirring, until mixture bubbles and is well browned. Gradually stir in juice; bring to a boil, stirring, until gravy boils and thickens. Strain gravy into same jug; serve turkey with cornbread stuffing and gravy.

MACERATED FRUIT Combine ingredients in small glass jar, cover; stand at room temperature for two days.

CORNBREAD STUFFING Line 7cm x 21cm loaf tin with baking parchment, extending it 5cm over long sides. Cook chorizo in large frying pan, stirring, until browned lightly. Add onion and shallot; cook, stirring, until onion softens. Add apple; cook, stirring, until browned lightly. Remove from heat; stir in sage, juice, cornbread and macerated fruit. Place stuffing in prepared tin in oven alongside turkey; cook, uncovered, in moderate oven during last 30 minutes of turkey roasting time.

ASIAN-SPICED TURKEY WITH CRANBERRY & PEACH CHUTNEY

You can ask your butcher to butterfly the turkey for you if you wish.

4kg turkey
2 tablespoons sichuan peppercorns
2 star anise
1 tablespoon coriander seeds
1 tablespoon cumin seeds
2 teaspoons salt
2 teaspoons dried chilli flakes
1 teaspoon ground ginger
1 teaspoon five-spice powder
⅓ cup (80ml) olive oil

CRANBERRY & PEACH CHUTNEY
7 large peaches (1.5kg)
1 cup (250ml) cider vinegar
¼ cup (60ml) lemon juice
1 cup (150g) dried cranberries
1 small brown onion (80g), chopped finely
½ teaspoon ground cinnamon
½ teaspoon ground cloves
½ teaspoon ground ginger
½ teaspoon ground allspice
2 cups (440g) caster sugar

PREPARATION TIME 25 MINUTES * COOKING TIME 2 HOURS * SERVES 8-12 (DEPENDING ON YOUR MENU)

1 Discard neck from turkey. Rinse turkey under cold water; pat dry inside and out with absorbent paper. Using kitchen scissors, cut along each side of turkey's backbone; discard backbone. Turn turkey skin-side up; using heel of hand, press down on breastbone to flatten turkey.
2 Using mortar and pestle, crush peppercorns, star anise, seeds and salt until mixture is crushed coarsely. Dry-fry peppercorn mixture with chilli, ginger and five-spice, in small frying pan, until fragrant. Remove from heat; stir in oil. Rub all over turkey.
3 Place turkey in a preheated moderate oven (180°C/160°C fan-forced) for about 2 hours or until cooked through.
4 Meanwhile, make cranberry and peach chutney.
5 Serve turkey with chutney.

CRANBERRY & PEACH CHUTNEY Place peaches in large bowl, cover with boiling water for 30 seconds; drain, peel, seed. Chop peaches coarsely, combine in medium saucepan with remaining ingredients; bring to a boil. Reduce heat; simmer, uncovered, stirring occasionally, about 1¼ hours or until chutney thickens.

TIP Chutney can be made up to three months ahead and stored in sterilised jars.

CHARGRILLED POULTRY PLATTER WITH LEMON DRESSING

PREPARATION TIME 20 MINUTES (PLUS REFRIGERATION TIME) * COOKING TIME 30 MINUTES * SERVES 8

4 duck breast fillets (800g), trimmed
2 fresh long red chillies, sliced thinly
8 chicken drumsticks (1.2kg)
2 x 500g spatchcocks, quartered
4 quails (800g), halved
⅓ cup (80ml) kecap manis (Indonesian sweet soy sauce)
¼ cup (90g) honey
300g cherry tomatoes on the vine
100g baby spinach leaves

LEMON DRESSING
1 teaspoon ground cumin
2 teaspoons ground coriander
½ cup (125ml) olive oil
¾ cup (180ml) lemon juice

1 Make lemon dressing.
2 Combine duck in medium bowl with ¼ cup of the dressing and half of the chilli; toss duck to coat in chilli marinade. Combine chicken, spatchcock and quail in large bowl with remaining dressing; toss to coat in lemon marinade. Cover each bowl; refrigerate 3 hours or overnight.
3 Drain duck over small bowl; reserve chilli marinade. Drain chicken, spatchcock and quail over medium bowl; reserve lemon marinade. Cook chicken, spatchcock and quail, in batches, on heated oiled grill plate (or grill) until cooked through. During cooking, brush chicken with reserved lemon marinade, spatchcock with ¼ cup of the kecap manis, and quail with honey. Brush duck with reserved chilli marinade; cook as desired.
4 Cook tomatoes on same heated oiled grill plate about 5 minutes or until just softened.
5 Cut duck into thick slices. Place spinach on large serving platter; arrange poultry and tomatoes on platter. Sprinkle duck with remaining chilli; drizzle spatchcock with remaining kecap manis.

LEMON DRESSING Dry-fry cumin and coriander in small heated frying pan, stirring, until fragrant. Combine spice mixture in small jug with oil and juice.

HONEY-GLAZED PORK
WITH SAGE

Ask your butcher to remove the rind completely from the pork loin and score it.

PREPARATION TIME 30 MINUTES *
COOKING TIME 2 HOURS 30 MINUTES
* SERVES 8

2.5kg boned loin of pork
2 teaspoons vegetable oil
1 tablespoon salt
2 cloves garlic, crushed
1 tablespoon finely chopped fresh sage
⅓ cup (90g) honey, warmed
1 tablespoon red wine vinegar
2 cups (500ml) chicken stock
2 tablespoons cornflour
2 tablespoons water

1 Preheat oven to very hot. Lay pork rind, fat-side down, on wire rack in large flameproof baking dish; rub oil and salt into it. Bake, uncovered, in very hot oven about 30 minutes or until the crackling is crisp and browned; cool. Discard fat from baking dish.

2 Lay pork, fat-side down, on board; sprinkle with half of the garlic and half of the sage. Roll pork to enclose sage and garlic; secure with kitchen string at 2cm intervals.

3 Place pork on wire rack in large flameproof baking dish. Reduce oven temperature to moderately hot; bake pork, uncovered, 30 minutes. Cover pork with foil, reduce oven temperature to moderate; bake 1 hour.

4 Combine honey, vinegar and remaining sage and garlic in small bowl. Remove foil from pork, brush pork with half of the honey mixture. Bake pork, uncovered, 30 minutes or until browned and cooked through, brushing occasionally with remaining honey mixture. Remove pork from dish; cover with foil.

5 Strain pan juices from baking dish into heatproof jug; remove fat from pan juices (you will need ⅔ cup of pan juices). Add stock to baking dish with pan juices. Stir in combined cornflour and water; stir until sauce boils and thickens. Serve pork slices with sauce and crackling.

honey-glazed pork with sage

RACK OF PORK
WITH APPLE SAUCE

Kipfler are small finger-shaped potatoes. You can use halved desirée or any other firm-fleshed potatoes if you prefer.

coarse salt
1.3kg pork rack (6 cutlets)
1.25kg kipfler potatoes
750g squash, chopped coarsely
1 tablespoon olive oil

APPLE SAUCE
3 large green apples (600g)
¼ cup (60ml) water
4 fresh sage leaves
1 teaspoon sugar

PREPARATION TIME 30 MINUTES *
COOKING TIME 1 HOUR 30 MINUTES
* SERVES 6

1 Preheat oven to very hot. Rub salt evenly into rind of pork. Cover bones with foil to prevent burning. Place pork, rind-side up, in large baking dish; bake, uncovered, in very hot oven about 35 minutes or until rind is blistered and browned.
2 Place potatoes and squash in separate baking dish, drizzle with oil. Reduce oven temperature to moderate; bake pork and vegetables, uncovered, about 40 minutes or until pork is cooked through. Remove pork from dish; cover with foil to keep warm.
3 Increase oven temperature to very hot; bake vegetables for 15 minutes or until browned and tender. Serve pork with vegetables and apple sauce.

APPLE SAUCE Peel and core apples; cut into thick slices. Combine apple, the water and sage in medium saucepan; simmer, uncovered, about 10 minutes or until apple is soft. Remove from heat, stir in sugar.

HERBED BEEF FILLET WITH HORSERADISH CREAM SAUCE

PREPARATION TIME 15 MINUTES *
COOKING TIME 40 MINUTES * SERVES 8

1 tablespoon finely grated
lemon rind
⅓ cup (80ml) lemon juice
1 teaspoon dried chilli flakes
3 cloves garlic, crushed
¼ cup coarsely chopped fresh
flat-leaf parsley
¼ cup loosely packed fresh
oregano leaves
¼ cup coarsely chopped
fresh basil
¼ cup loosely packed fresh
marjoram leaves
⅓ cup (80ml) olive oil
2kg piece beef tenderloin

HORSERADISH CREAM SAUCE
1 tablespoon olive oil
2 cloves garlic, crushed
2 teaspoons plain flour
½ cup (125ml) dry white wine
½ cup (140g) horseradish cream
600ml cream

1 Preheat oven to moderately hot.
2 Combine rind, juice, chilli, garlic, herbs and oil in large bowl, add beef; roll beef to coat in herb mixture. Place beef on oiled wire rack in large shallow baking dish. Roast, uncovered, in moderately hot oven about 40 minutes or until cooked as desired. Cover beef; stand 10 minutes.
3 Meanwhile, make horseradish cream sauce.
4 Serve sliced beef with sauce.

HORSERADISH CREAM SAUCE Heat oil in small frying pan; cook garlic and flour, stirring, until mixtures bubbles and browns lightly. Gradually stir in wine; bring to a boil, stirring. Reduce heat; simmer, uncovered, until liquid reduces by half. Stir in horseradish and cream; simmer, stirring, about 5 minutes or until sauce thickens slightly.

SPICED BEEF
WITH CHILLI JAM

PREPARATION TIME 20 MINUTES *
COOKING TIME 45 MINUTES * SERVES 4

1 tablespoon cumin seeds
1 tablespoon coriander seeds
1 teaspoon cardamom seeds
750g beef eye fillet

CHILLI JAM
2 tablespoons olive oil
2 medium red peppers (400g), chopped
2 small tomatoes (260g), chopped
3 small brown onions (300g), chopped
4 red thai chillies, deseeded, chopped
3 cloves garlic, crushed
½ cup (125ml) white wine vinegar
½ cup (110g) caster sugar
¼ cup (50g) brown sugar
1 tablespoon balsamic vinegar

1 Place seeds in a dry frying pan; stir over low heat until fragrant. Grind or blend spices until crushed.
2 Roll beef in spices, cover; refrigerate beef 3 hours or overnight.
3 Preheat oven to moderate. Place beef in oiled baking dish; bake, uncovered, in moderate oven about 45 minutes or until cooked as desired. Stand, covered, 10 minutes before carving.
4 Serve beef with chilli jam.

CHILLI JAM Heat oil in large saucepan, add pepper, tomato, onion, chilli and garlic; cook, stirring, over low heat, about 20 minutes or until pepper is soft. Add white wine vinegar and caster sugar; stir over heat, without boiling, until sugar dissolves. Simmer, uncovered, about 15 minutes or until mixture is thick. Stir in brown sugar and balsamic vinegar; blend or process mixture until roughly chopped. Spoon into hot sterilised jar, seal while hot; cool, refrigerate.

MIDDLE-EASTERN LAMB WITH OLIVE COUSCOUS STUFFING

Ask your butcher to butterfly the leg of lamb for you.

2kg leg of lamb, butterflied
1 tablespoon olive oil
⅓ cup (80ml) orange juice
½ teaspoon ground cinnamon
¼ cup (90g) honey
2 cloves garlic, crushed
1½ tablespoons cornflour
2 cups (500ml) beef stock

OLIVE COUSCOUS STUFFING
½ cup (100g) couscous
½ cup (125ml) boiling water
20g butter
1 small white onion (80g), chopped finely
1 teaspoon ground cumin
2 tablespoons flaked almonds, toasted
1 small apple (130g), peeled, cored, chopped coarsely
1 tablespoon brown sugar
¼ cup (40g) coarsely chopped stoned black olives

PREPARATION TIME 30 MINUTES * COOKING TIME 1 HOUR 30 MINUTES * SERVES 6

1 Preheat oven to moderate.
2 Place lamb on board, pound with meat mallet until lamb is an even thickness. Place olive couscous stuffing in centre of lamb; roll up from short side to enclose stuffing.
3 Secure lamb with skewers, tie with kitchen string at 2cm intervals. Place lamb on wire rack in baking dish, brush with oil. Bake, uncovered, in moderate oven 1 hour.
4 Combine juice, cinnamon, honey and garlic in small bowl; brush a little juice mixture over lamb. Return lamb to moderate oven for 30 minutes or until tender; baste with remaining juice mixture several times during cooking. Remove lamb from dish; stand, covered, 10 minutes before carving.
5 Meanwhile, blend cornflour with a little of the stock in small bowl; stir into juices in baking dish with remaining stock. Stir over heat until mixture boils and thickens; strain. Serve with lamb.

OLIVE COUSCOUS STUFFING Combine couscous and the water in heatproof bowl; stand, covered, 5 minutes or until all the liquid has been absorbed. Meanwhile, heat butter in small frying pan, add onion; cook, stirring, until soft. Add cumin, nuts, apple, sugar and olives; cook, stirring, about 3 minutes or until apple is softened slightly. Stir in couscous; cool.

BONED SHOULDER OF LAMB WITH CORIANDER HAZELNUT PESTO

Ask the butcher to bone the lamb shoulder for you.

PREPARATION TIME 20 MINUTES • COOKING TIME 1 HOUR 45 MINUTES • SERVES 6

⅓ cup (50g) unroasted hazelnuts
½ cup firmly packed fresh
coriander leaves
⅓ cup firmly packed fresh basil leaves
1 tablespoon grated fresh ginger
5 cloves garlic, crushed
2 tablespoons lime juice
2 teaspoons fish sauce
1 teaspoon brown sugar
2 tablespoons olive oil
1.7kg lamb shoulder, boned

1 Preheat oven to moderately hot. Spread nuts in a single layer on oven tray; toast, uncovered, in moderately hot oven about 5 minutes or until skins begin to flake. Rub hazelnuts in soft cloth to remove skins; cool.
2 Reduce oven temperature to moderate. Blend or process nuts, herbs, ginger, garlic, juice, sauce and sugar until pureed. With motor operating, pour in oil; process until pesto thickens.
3 Spread lamb with half of the pesto. Roll from short side to enclose pesto; secure lamb with skewers, tie with kitchen string at 2cm intervals.
4 Place lamb on wire rack in large baking dish. Spread remaining pesto onto outside of lamb.
5 Bake, uncovered, in moderate oven about 1¾ hours or until cooked as desired. Stand lamb, covered, 10 minutes before carving.

FIG & ORANGE GLAZED HAM

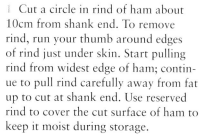

PREPARATION TIME 20 MINUTES
* COOKING TIME 1 HOUR
15 MINUTES * SERVES 16

8kg cooked leg ham
60 whole cloves (approx.)

FIG & ORANGE GLAZE
1 cup (320g) fig jam
2 tablespoons dijon mustard
⅓ cup (80ml) orange juice
2 tablespoons brandy

1 Cut a circle in rind of ham about 10cm from shank end. To remove rind, run your thumb around edges of rind just under skin. Start pulling rind from widest edge of ham; continue to pull rind carefully away from fat up to cut at shank end. Use reserved rind to cover the cut surface of ham to keep it moist during storage.

2 Preheat oven to moderate. Using a sharp knife, score across fat at about 3cm intervals, cutting just through surface of fat. Do not cut deeply into fat, or it will spread apart during cooking. Score in opposite direction to make a diamond pattern; stud with cloves.

4 Place ham on wire rack in large baking dish; cover shank with foil. Brush ham with half of the fig and orange glaze; bake, uncovered, in moderate oven about 1¼ hours or until browned, brushing often with remaining glaze during cooking.

FIG & ORANGE GLAZE Combine jam, mustard, juice and brandy in small saucepan; stir over low heat, without boiling, until jam melts.

blood orange marmalade
glazed ham

BLOOD ORANGE
MARMALADE GLAZED HAM

This recipe can be prepared several hours ahead. For delicious hot ham, serve soon after glazing. Carved ham is suitable to freeze for up to 1 month (ham will become saltier if frozen longer).

9kg cooked leg of ham
whole cloves, to decorate

BLOOD ORANGE
MARMALADE GLAZE
350g jar blood orange
marmalade
¼ cup (55g) brown sugar
¼ cup (60ml) orange juice

PREPARATION TIME 20 MINUTES * COOKING TIME
1 HOUR 30 MINUTES *

1 Preheat the oven to moderate (180°C/160°C fan-forced). Cut through the rind of the ham about 10cm from the shank end of the leg.
2 To remove the rind, run your thumb around the edge of the rind, just under the skin. Start pulling the rind from the widest edge of the ham; continue to pull the rind carefully away from the fat up to the cut. Remove the rind completely. (Reserved rind can be used to cover the cut surface of the ham to keep it moist during storage.)
3 Using a sharp knife, score across the fat very lightly at about 3cm intervals, cutting just through the surface of the top fat. Don't cut too deeply or the fat will spread apart during cooking. Score in the opposite direction to form a diamond pattern.
4 Line a large baking dish with overlapping sheets of baking parchment (this will make cleaning the dish easier). Place the ham on a wire rack in the baking dish. Brush ham well with the blood orange marmalade glaze and cover the shank end with foil.
5 Bake in a moderate oven for 40 minutes. Decorate the ham with the cloves. Bake for a further 40 minutes or until browned all over, brushing occasionally with the glaze during cooking.
6 Serve warm or cold.

BLOOD ORANGE MARMALADE GLAZE Combine all ingredients in a small saucepan, stir over a low heat until the sugar is dissolved.

ASIAN-STYLE BAKED HAM

PREPARATION TIME 15 MINUTES (PLUS
REFRIGERATION TIME) * COOKING TIME
1 HOUR 30 MINUTES * SERVES 8–12
(DEPENDING ON YOUR MENU)

7kg cooked leg of ham
1 cup (250ml) soy sauce
¾ cup (180ml) dry sherry
⅓ cup (75g) firmly packed
brown sugar
⅓ cup (120g) honey
2 teaspoons red food
colouring
4 cloves garlic, crushed
2 teaspoons five-spice
powder
60 cloves (approx.)

1 Cut through rind about 10cm from shank end
of leg in decorative pattern; run thumb around
edge of rind just under skin to remove rind. Start
pulling rind from shank end to widest edge of
ham; discard rind.

2 Using sharp knife, make shallow cuts in one
direction diagonally across fat at 3cm intervals,
then shallow-cut in opposite direction, forming
diamonds. Do not cut through top fat or fat will
spread apart during cooking.

3 Combine soy, sherry, sugar, honey, colouring,
garlic and five-spice in small bowl. Place ham on
wire rack in large baking dish; brush ham with
soy mixture. Centre a clove in each diamond
shape, cover; refrigerate overnight.

4 Preheat oven to moderate.

5 Place ham on wire rack in large baking dish;
pour marinade into small jug. Cover ham with
greased foil; bake in moderate oven 1 hour.
Uncover; bake in moderate oven about 30 minutes or until ham is lightly caramelised, brushing
frequently with marinade during cooking.

TIP As an alternative to the Asian flavours used
above, a glaze of orange, ginger and maple syrup
also goes beautifully with this ham. Combine
1 cup maple syrup, 1 cup fresh orange juice,
⅓ cup orange marmalade, ¼ cup grated fresh
ginger and 2 teaspoons finely grated orange rind
in small saucepan; bring to a boil. Reduce heat;
simmer, uncovered, 15 minutes then strain before
brushing over ham during baking.

Straight to the sauce

A good sauce can turn a plain roast into something sublime. These recipes will ensure your roasts are unforgettable.

GRAVY

MAKES 2 CUPS (500ML)

1 small brown onion (80g), chopped finely
2 tablespoons plain flour
½ cup (125ml) dry red wine
1½ cups (375ml) chicken or beef stock

1 Remove roast from baking dish, cover to keep warm. Reserve 2 tablespoons of juices in baking dish; discard remaining juice.
2 Add onion to dish; cook, stirring, until soft. Stir in flour; cook, stirring, about 5 minutes or until browned. Pour in wine and stock; cook over high heat, stirring, until gravy boils and thickens. Strain gravy before serving.

TIP To adapt this gravy into peppercorn or mushroom gravy, place strained gravy in small saucepan; add 1 tablespoon drained canned green peppercorns or 100g finely sliced cooked button mushrooms. Cook, stirring, for 2 minutes.

DEVILLED SAUCE

MAKES 2 CUPS (500ML)

1 tablespoon olive oil
1 medium brown onion (150g), chopped finely
2 cloves garlic, crushed
1 teaspoon hot paprika
¼ cup (50g) firmly packed brown sugar
⅓ cup (80ml) cider vinegar
1 teaspoon Tabasco sauce
1 tablespoon Worcestershire sauce
2 cups (500ml) beef stock
1 tablespoon cornflour
1 tablespoon water

1 Heat oil in medium frying pan, add onion and garlic; cook, stirring, until onion is soft. Stir in paprika, sugar and vinegar; cook, stirring, without boiling, until sugar dissolves.
2 Add sauces and stock; simmer, uncovered, about 15 minutes or until reduced to 2 cups. Stir in blended cornflour and water; stir until sauce boils and thickens.

TRADITIONAL MINT SAUCE

MAKES 1¼ CUPS (310ML)

1 cup (250ml) cider vinegar
¼ cup (60ml) boiling water
¼ cup finely chopped fresh mint leaves
1 tablespoon brown sugar
1 teaspoon salt
¼ teaspoon ground black pepper

1 Combine ingredients in small bowl; stand 30 minutes before serving.

APPLE SAUCE

MAKES 1 CUP (250ML)

2 small apples (260g)
2 tablespoons sugar
½ cup (125ml) water
pinch ground cinnamon

1 Peel apples; cut into quarters. Remove core; slice apple.
2 Combine apple, sugar, the water and cinnamon in small saucepan, cover; bring to a boil. Reduce heat; simmer, covered, about 5 minutes or until apple is pulpy. Whisk until sauce is smooth.

SALT-CRUSTED OCEAN TROUT WITH THAI-FLAVOURS HOLLANDAISE

Cooking salt is coarser than table salt, but not as large-flaked as sea salt: it is sold packaged in bags in most supermarkets. You'll need a very large (approximately 30cm x 40cm) baking dish in order to fit in the whole fish.

2kg cooking salt
3 egg whites
2.4kg whole ocean trout

THAI-FLAVOURS
HOLLANDAISE
10cm stick (20g) fresh
lemon grass
2 tablespoons water
½ cup (125ml) white
wine vinegar
1 tablespoon lemon juice
1 teaspoon black
peppercorns
1 tablespoon finely chopped
fresh lemon grass
6 egg yolks
250g butter, melted
2 tablespoons lime juice
4 fresh kaffir lime leaves,
shredded finely

PREPARATION TIME 20 MINUTES * COOKING TIME 1 HOUR 15 MINUTES * SERVES 8

1 Preheat oven to moderately hot.
2 Combine salt with egg whites in medium bowl (mixture will resemble wet sand). Spread about half of the salt mixture evenly over base of shallow 30cm x 40cm baking dish; place fish on salt mixture then cover completely (except for tail) with remaining salt mixture. Cook fish in moderately hot oven 1 hour.
3 Meanwhile, make thai-flavours hollandaise.
4 Remove fish from oven; break salt crust with heavy knife, taking care not to cut into fish. Discard salt crust; transfer fish to large serving platter.
5 Carefully remove skin from fish; flake fish into large pieces. Serve fish with hollandaise.

THAI-FLAVOURS HOLLANDAISE Bruise lemon grass stick with side of heavy knife. Combine lemon grass stick with the water, vinegar, juice and peppercorns in small saucepan; bring to a boil. Reduce heat; simmer, uncovered, until mixture reduces to 2 tablespoons. Discard lemon grass stick; stir in chopped lemon grass; cool 10 minutes. Combine vinegar mixture with egg yolks in medium heatproof bowl over medium saucepan of simmering water; whisk mixture constantly about 5 minutes or until thickened. Gradually add butter in thin, steady stream, whisking constantly until mixture thickens. Whisk in juice and lime leaves.

SLOW-ROASTED SALMON

PREPARATION TIME 10 MINUTES *
COOKING TIME 35 MINUTES * SERVES 4

750g piece salmon fillet,
boned, with skin on
1 tablespoon finely shredded
kaffir lime leaves
¼ cup (55g) caster sugar
2 tablespoons lime juice
2 tablespoons water
1 fresh red thai chilli,
deseeded, chopped finely
1 tablespoon coarsely
chopped fresh coriander

1 Preheat oven to very slow. Cook fish on heated oiled grill plate until browned both sides. Place fish in large oiled baking dish, sprinkle with lime leaves; bake, covered tightly, in very slow oven about 30 minutes or until cooked as desired.
2 Meanwhile, combine sugar, juice and the water in small saucepan; stir over heat, without boiling, until sugar dissolves. Simmer, uncovered, without stirring, 2 minutes; cool slightly, stir in chilli and coriander.
3 Serve fish drizzled with chilli sauce.

slow-roasted salmon

SLOW-ROASTED PESTO SALMON

PREPARATION TIME 20 MINUTES *
COOKING TIME 45 MINUTES * SERVES 8

1 cup loosely packed fresh
basil leaves
2 cloves garlic, chopped
coarsely
2 tablespoons toasted
pine nuts
2 tablespoons lemon juice
¼ cup (60ml) olive oil
1.5kg piece salmon fillet,
skin on
2 tablespoons olive oil, extra
2 large red peppers (700g),
chopped coarsely
1 large red onion (300g),
chopped coarsely

1 Preheat oven to moderately slow.
2 Blend or process basil, garlic, nuts and juice until combined. With motor operating, gradually add oil in thin, steady stream until pesto thickens slightly.
3 Place fish, skin-side down, on piece of lightly oiled foil large enough to completely enclose fish; coat fish with half of the pesto. Gather corners of foil together above fish; twist to enclose securely. Place parcel on oven tray; roast in moderately slow oven about 45 minutes or until cooked as desired.
4 Meanwhile, heat extra oil in large frying pan; cook pepper and onion, stirring, until onion softens.
5 Place fish parcel on serving platter, unwrap; top with onion mixture, drizzle with remaining pesto.

TIP If the pesto is a little too thick for your liking, thin it down with a little olive oil before drizzling over the salmon.

VEGETABLES

WARM POTATO SALAD WITH CAPERBERRIES

PREPARATION TIME 10 MINUTES *
COOKING TIME 15 MINUTES * SERVES 8

2kg firm-fleshed potatoes, unpeeled, diced into
2cm pieces
1 tablespoon dijon mustard
2 tablespoons red wine vinegar
½ cup (125ml) extra virgin olive oil
1 small white onion (80g), sliced thinly
¼ cup firmly packed fresh flat-leaf parsley leaves
2 tablespoons fresh dill sprigs
1 cup (200g) cornichons, halved lengthways
½ cup (80g) drained large caperberries, rinsed

1 Boil, steam or microwave potato until just
tender; drain.
2 Meanwhile, whisk mustard, vinegar and oil
in large bowl until combined. Add hot potato
to bowl with onion, herbs, cornichons and caperberries; toss gently to combine.

warm potato salad
with caperberries

TRADITIONAL ROAST POTATOES

PREPARATION TIME 15 MINUTES * COOKING TIME 1 HOUR 5 MINUTES * SERVES 4

5 medium potatoes (1kg)
2 tablespoons olive oil
40g butter, melted
1 teaspoon salt

1 Preheat oven to hot. Cut potatoes into uniformly-sized pieces.
2 Cook potato in large saucepan of boiling water 5 minutes. Drain; cool on absorbent paper.
3 Combine potato, oil and butter in large baking dish. Sprinkle with salt; bake in hot oven about 1 hour or until tender.

PERFECT ROAST POTATOES

PREPARATION TIME 15 MINUTES *
COOKING TIME 55 MINUTES * SERVES 8

12 medium desirée potatoes
(2.5kg), halved lengthways
⅓ cup (80ml) olive oil

1 Preheat oven to hot. Oil oven tray.
2 Boil, steam or microwave potato 5 minutes; drain. Pat dry with absorbent paper; cool for 10 minutes.
3 Rake rounded sides of potato gently with tines of fork; place potato, cut-side down, in single layer, on prepared tray. Brush with oil; roast, uncovered, in hot oven about 50 minutes or until potato is browned lightly and crisp.

MEDITERRANEAN POTATO MASH

PREPARATION TIME 25 MINUTES *
COOKING TIME 20 MINUTES * SERVES 8

2.5kg red-skinned potatoes, chopped coarsely
100g butter, softened
1½ cups (375ml) hot milk
½ cup (75g) drained sun-dried tomatoes, chopped coarsely
¼ cup coarsely chopped fresh flat-leaf parsley

BALSAMIC DRESSING
¼ cup (60ml) balsamic vinegar
2 tablespoons olive oil

1 Boil, steam or microwave potato until tender; drain.
2 Meanwhile, make balsamic dressing.
3 Mash potato in large bowl with butter and milk until smooth. Stir in tomato and parsley.
4 Serve mash drizzled with dressing.

BALSAMIC DRESSING Place ingredients in screw-top jar; shake well.

mediterranean potato mash

*mustard &
honey glazed
sweet potatoes*

MUSTARD & HONEY-GLAZED ROASTED SWEET POTATOES

PREPARATION TIME 10 MINUTES ✳
COOKING TIME 1 HOUR✳ SERVES 8

2.5kg sweet potatoes,
unpeeled
⅔ cup (240g) honey
⅓ cup (95g) wholegrain
mustard
2 tablespoons coarsely
chopped fresh rosemary

1 Preheat oven to hot.
2 Halve sweet potatoes lengthways; cut each half into 2cm wedges.
3 Combine remaining ingredients in large bowl, add sweet potatoes; toss sweet potatoes to coat in mixture. Divide sweet potato mixture between two large shallow baking dishes. Roast, uncovered, in hot oven about 1 hour or until sweet potatoes are tender and slightly caramelised.

GARLIC & ROSEMARY
ROASTED VEGETABLES

PREPARATION TIME 10 MINUTES * COOKING
TIME 1 HOUR 30 MINUTES * SERVES 8

3 small round pumpkins or
baby turnips (1.2kg)
1.5kg baby new potatoes
800g spring onions, trimmed
8 cloves garlic, unpeeled
2 tablespoons olive oil
¼ cup fresh rosemary

1 Preheat oven to moderate. Cut pumpkins into
quarters; remove and discard seeds. Cut each
quarter in half.
2 Combine pumpkin, potatoes, onion, garlic, oil
and half of the rosemary in large baking dish;
bake in moderate oven about 1½ hours or until
vegetables are browned and tender. Serve roasted
vegetables sprinkled with remaining rosemary.

ROASTED GARLIC CELERIAC

PREPARATION TIME
10 MINUTES • COOKING
TIME 1 HOUR • SERVES 4

1 large celeriac (1.5kg)
2 tablespoons olive oil
1 medium bulb garlic (70g)
⅓ cup coarsely chopped fresh
flat-leaf parsley
⅓ cup (95g) low-fat plain
yogurt

1 Preheat oven to moderate.
Peel celeriac, cut into 3cm
chunks; combine with oil in
large bowl.
2 Place celeriac and unpeeled
garlic bulb on baking-paper-
lined oven tray; bake in moderate oven, turning occasionally,
about 1 hour or until celeriac is
tender and golden brown.
3 Cut garlic bulb in half
horizontally, squeeze garlic pulp
from each clove over celeriac;
toss together with parsley. Serve
celeriac topped with yogurt.

BALSAMIC-GLAZED BABY ONIONS

PREPARATION TIME 10 MINUTES
• COOKING TIME 15 MINUTES •
SERVES 8

1 tablespoon balsamic vinegar
1 tablespoon wholegrain mustard
¼ cup (90g) honey
2 tablespoons vegetable oil
500g baby onions, halved

1 Combine vinegar, mustard and honey
in small saucepan; bring to a boil.
Reduce heat; simmer, uncovered, about
5 minutes or until glaze thickens.
2 Heat oil in large frying pan; cook
onion, brushing constantly with glaze,
stirring, until browned and cooked as
desired.

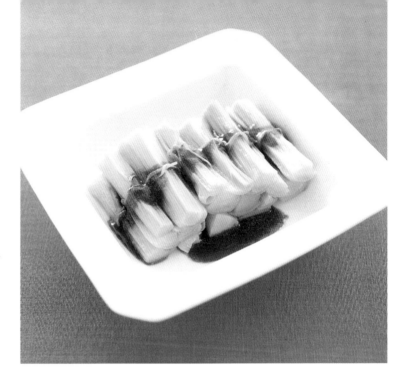

LEEKS IN VINAIGRETTE

PREPARATION TIME 20 MINUTES •
COOKING TIME 35 MINUTES • SERVES 8

4 medium leeks (1.4kg)
50g butter, chopped
⅓ cup (80ml) dry white wine
3 cups (750ml) chicken stock

RASPBERRY VINAIGRETTE
150g raspberries
¼ cup (60ml) raspberry vinegar
2 tablespoons olive oil

1 Preheat oven to moderate. Discard root end; trim green
section to leave 14cm leek. Remove outer layer of each leek;
cut outer layer lengthways into thin strips. Soften strips in
saucepan of boiling water; drain.
2 Halve leeks crossways; quarter each piece lengthways.
Tie each quarter in the centre with a few leek strips.
3 Combine butter, wine and stock in large baking dish;
place leeks in stock mixture. Cook, covered, in moderate
oven about 25 minutes or until leeks are tender.
4 Meanwhile, make vinaigrette; drizzle over leeks.

RASPBERRY VINAIGRETTE Push berries through sieve into
small bowl; discard seeds. Whisk in vinegar and oil.

BROCCOLINI POLONAISE

*A 'polonaise', the French interpretation of a
classic Polish way of presenting cooked vegetables
such as cauliflower, broccoli, asparagus and the
like, is a topping of chopped or sieved hard-boiled
egg, buttered breadcrumbs and chopped parsley.*

PREPARATION TIME 10 MINUTES *
COOKING TIME 10 MINUTES * SERVES 8

60g butter
1 cup (70g) stale breadcrumbs
4 hard-boiled eggs,
chopped finely
¼ cup finely chopped fresh
flat-leaf parsley
750g broccolini
60g butter, melted

1 Melt butter in large frying pan; cook breadcrumbs, stirring, until browned and crisp.
Combine breadcrumbs in small bowl with egg
and parsley.
2 Boil, steam or microwave broccolini until just
tender; drain.
3 Top broccolini with polonaise mixture then
drizzle with the melted butter.

BABY CARROTS WITH ORANGE MAPLE SYRUP

PREPARATION TIME 35 MINUTES
* COOKING TIME 20 MINUTES *
SERVES 8

1.6kg baby carrots
30g butter
2 teaspoons finely grated orange rind
2 tablespoons orange juice
2 tablespoons maple syrup

1 Boil, steam or microwave carrots until just tender.
2 Melt butter in large frying pan; stir rind, juice and syrup in pan until mixture boils. Reduce heat; simmer, uncovered, until syrup mixture thickens slightly. Add drained carrots to pan, stirring gently to coat in orange maple syrup.

PEAS WITH CARAWAY & PARMESAN

60g butter
1 teaspoon caraway seeds
2 teaspoons finely grated lemon rind
1 small red onion (100g), sliced thinly
4 cups (640g) peas
⅓ cup coarsely chopped fresh flat-leaf parsley
½ cup (40g) finely grated parmesan cheese

PREPARATION TIME 35 MINUTES *
COOKING TIME 5 MINUTES * SERVES 8

1 Melt butter in large frying pan; cook seeds, rind and onion, stirring, until onion softens.
2 Add peas; cook, stirring, until peas are just tender. Stir in parsley; sprinkle with cheese.

PEAS & BEANS
WITH HAZELNUTS

This recipe can prepared a day ahead; cook just before serving.

PREPARATION TIME 15 MINUTES *
COOKING TIME 12 MINUTES * SERVES 8

1½ cups (240g) peas
300g baby beans, trimmed
300g sugar snap peas, trimmed
30g butter
⅓ cup (35g) roasted hazelnuts, chopped coarsely
1 clove garlic, crushed
salt and freshly ground black pepper

1 Boil or steam the peas and beans until almost tender; add the sugar snap peas, cook for a further 30 seconds or until just tender; drain well.
2 Melt butter in a large frying pan; cook nuts until browned. Remove nuts from pan with a slotted spoon. Add garlic then vegetables to pan; toss until combined. Season to taste with salt and pepper.
3 Serve vegetables topped with nuts.

sesame patty-pan squash
& sugar snap peas

SESAME PATTY-PAN SQUASH & SUGAR SNAP PEAS

PREPARATION TIME 5 MINUTES
* COOKING TIME 10 MINUTES *
SERVES 8

16 yellow patty-pan squash (480g)
300g sugar snap peas, trimmed
2 teaspoons sesame oil
1 tablespoon soy sauce
1 tablespoon toasted sesame seeds

1 Boil, steam or microwave squash and peas, separately, until tender; drain.
2 Place vegetables in large bowl with remaining ingredients; toss gently to combine.

BARBECUED CORN, BROAD BEANS & PEPPERS

PREPARATION TIME 20 MINUTES *
COOKING TIME 15 MINUTES * SERVES 8

4 trimmed corn cobs (1kg)
500g frozen broad beans, thawed, peeled
1 medium red pepper (200g), chopped finely
20g butter

1 Cook corn on heated oiled grill plate (or grill) until just tender. When cool enough to handle, use a sharp knife to cut kernels from cobs.
2 Meanwhile, boil, steam or microwave broad beans until tender; drain.
3 Place corn and beans in large bowl with remaining ingredients; toss gently to combine.

ROASTED PEPPERS WITH PORT & BASIL DRESSING

2 medium red peppers (400g)
2 medium green peppers (400g)
2 medium yellow peppers (400g)
10 green onions
8 cloves garlic
4 small white onions (400g), quartered
1 tablespoon olive oil

PORT & BASIL DRESSING
½ cup (125ml) olive oil
¼ cup (60ml) balsamic vinegar
2 cloves garlic
⅓ cup firmly packed fresh basil leaves
1 tablespoon port
1 tablespoon mild chilli sauce

PREPARATION TIME 10 MINUTES • COOKING TIME
1 HOUR • SERVES 8

1 Preheat oven to moderate.
2 Quarter peppers; remove and discard seeds and membranes. Combine with remaining ingredients in large baking dish; bake, uncovered, in moderate oven 1 hour.
3 Serve warm pepper mixture with port and basil dressing.

PORT & BASIL DRESSING Blend or process ingredients until pureed.

ROASTED MUSHROOMS

PREPARATION TIME 10 MINUTES
• COOKING TIME 20 MINUTES •
SERVES 6

500g button mushrooms
500g chestnut mushrooms
3 cloves garlic, crushed
2 tablespoons olive oil
2 teaspoons salt
½ teaspoon freshly ground black pepper

1 Preheat oven to hot. Combine ingredients in large bowl; place mixture in single layer in baking dish.
2 Bake, uncovered, in hot oven about 20 minutes or until mushrooms are very soft and browned lightly.

BABY BEETROOT
WITH CAPER VINAIGRETTE

You need approximately two bunches of baby beetroot for this recipe.

1kg baby beetroot
1 tablespoon drained baby capers, rinsed
2 tablespoons white wine vinegar
2 tablespoons olive oil
1 teaspoon dijon mustard

PREPARATION TIME 10 MINUTES *
COOKING TIME 20 MINUTES * SERVES 8

1 Remove stems from beetroot; cook beetroot in large saucepan of boiling water, uncovered, about 20 minutes or until tender. Drain; cool 10 minutes. Peel beetroot.
2 Place beetroot in large bowl with remaining ingredients; toss gently to combine.

ROASTED BEETROOT & ONION

PREPARATION TIME 10 MINUTES • COOKING TIME
1 HOUR 25 MINUTES • SERVES 6

2 tablespoons olive oil
10 medium unpeeled fresh
beetroot (1.6kg), halved
20 baby onions (500g), peeled
2 tablespoons red wine vinegar
2 tablespoons olive oil, extra
freshly ground black pepper
2 tablespoons coarsely chopped
fresh flat-leaf parsley

1 Preheat oven to very hot.
2 Brush base of baking dish with half of the oil, add beetroot;
cover tightly with foil. Bake in very hot oven 45 minutes.
3 Combine onions with remaining oil. Add onions to
beetroot in dish; cover tightly with foil. Bake in very hot oven
30 minutes or until vegetables are tender. Remove foil; cook
10 minutes.
4 Wearing rubber gloves, remove skin from hot beetroot.
Cut beetroot in half. Place beetroot and onion in serving dish;
drizzle with combined vinegar and extra oil, sprinkle with
pepper and parsley.

ROASTED TOMATOES
WITH BALSAMIC DRESSING

PREPARATION TIME 5 MINUTES · COOKING
TIME 1 HOUR 30 MINUTES · SERVES 6

12 large plum tomatoes (1kg),
halved lengthways
⅓ cup (80ml) olive oil
1 tablespoon sugar
2 cloves garlic, crushed
1 teaspoon salt
1 teaspoon cracked black pepper
1 tablespoon balsamic vinegar
1 tablespoon shredded fresh
basil leaves

1 Preheat oven to moderate.
2 Place tomato, cut-side up, on wire rack in
baking dish. Brush with half of the combined oil,
sugar, garlic, salt and pepper.
3 Bake, uncovered, in moderate oven about
1½ hours or until tomato is softened and
browned lightly.
4 Drizzle combined remaining oil and vinegar
over tomatoes; scatter with basil.

ROASTED VINE TOMATOES
WITH CRISPY BASIL LEAVES

PREPARATION TIME 10 MINUTES *
COOKING TIME 10 MINUTES * SERVES 8

500g cherry tomatoes
on the vine
2 cloves garlic, sliced thinly
1 tablespoon olive oil
2 teaspoons balsamic vinegar
vegetable oil, for deep-frying
⅓ cup loosely packed
fresh basil leaves

1 Preheat oven to moderate.
2 Place tomatoes on oven tray; pour combined garlic, oil and vinegar over tomatoes. Roast, uncovered, in moderate oven about 10 minutes or until tomatoes soften.
3 Meanwhile, heat vegetable oil in small saucepan; deep-fry basil, in batches, until crisp.
4 Serve tomatoes sprinkled with basil.

LEFTOVERS

TURKEY RILLETTES

PREPARATION TIME 15 MINUTES ∗
COOKING TIME 5 MINUTES ∗ SERVES 4

100g butter
⅓ cup cream
¼ teaspoon hot paprika
2 cups (320g) coarsely
chopped cooked turkey meat
½ small red onion, coarsely
chopped
¼ cup loosely packed fresh
flat-leaf parsley leaves

1 Melt butter with cream and paprika in small saucepan, stirring over low heat, until combined.
2 Blend or process cooked turkey meat, onion and flat-leaf parsley, pulsing, while adding butter mixture in thin, steady stream.
3 Place rillette mixture in four ½-cup (125ml) dishes, cover; refrigerate until required. Serve with pickled onions, olives and thinly sliced toasted french bread stick.

turkey rillettes

VIETNAMESE TURKEY SALAD

150g mangetout, trimmed
½ cucumber, deseeded and
cut into matchsticks
1 medium carrot cut into
matchsticks
1 small red pepper, thinly sliced
100g mangetout tendrils
½ cup loosely packed fresh
mint leaves
½ cup loosely packed fresh
coriander leaves
2 cups (320g) thinly sliced
turkey meat
2 tablespoons peanut oil
2 tablespoons lime juice
1 tablespoon brown sugar
1 tablespoon fish sauce
2 tablespoons coarsely chopped
unsalted roasted peanuts

PREPARATION TIME 20 MINUTES *
COOKING TIME 2 MINUTES * SERVES 4

1 Boil, steam or microwave mangetout until
just tender; drain. Immediately rinse under cold
water; drain.
2 Slice mangetout thinly lengthways; place in
large bowl with cucumber, carrot, red pepper,
mangetout tendrils, mint, coriander and turkey
meat.
3 Place peanut oil, lime juice, brown sugar and
fish sauce in screw-top jar; shake well.
4 Drizzle dressing over salad; toss gently to
combine, sprinkle with chopped peanuts.

HAM & EGG SLICE

2 teaspoons olive oil
2 medium brown onions,
thinly sliced
2 cloves garlic, crushed
2 cups (360g) finely chopped
cooked ham
6 eggs
300ml cream
½ cup finely grated
parmesan cheese
¼ cup finely chopped
fresh basil

PREPARATION TIME 15 MINUTES * COOKING
TIME 35 MINUTES * SERVES 8

1 Preheat oven to moderately low. Oil and line
base of 20cm x 30cm shallow baking tin.
2 Heat olive oil in medium frying pan; cook onions and garlic, stirring, until onion softens. Cool
for 5 minutes.
3 Combine onion mixture in large bowl with
ham, eggs, cream, parmesan cheese and basil;
pour mixture into prepared tin.
4 Bake, uncovered, in moderately slow oven
about 30 minutes or until set.

SALMON, PEA
& MINT LINGUINE

PREPARATION TIME 10 MINUTES *
COOKING TIME 15 MINUTES * SERVES 4

375g linguine (or any
long flat pasta)
1 medium brown onion,
finely chopped
1 clove garlic, crushed
½ cup chicken stock
½ cup water
¼ cup dry white wine
1 cup (120g) frozen peas
2 cups (400g) flaked
cooked salmon
⅓ cup coarsely chopped
fresh mint

1 Cook linguine in large saucepan of boiling water, uncovered, until just tender.
2 Meanwhile, cook onion and garlic in oiled large frying pan until onion softens.
3 Add chicken stock, water and wine, reduce heat; simmer, uncovered, until liquid reduces by one third.
4 Add peas, salmon and mint; stir until just heated through. Add to drained pasta; toss gently to combine.

turkey salad
sandwiches

TURKEY SALAD SANDWICHES

**PREPARATION TIME 15 MINUTES
* SERVES 4**

1 cup (150g) finely chopped
cooked turkey meat
1 celery stalk, trimmed and finely
chopped
30g baby rocket leaves,
finely chopped
2 tablespoons toasted slivered
almonds, coarsely chopped
¼ cup sour cream
¼ cup whole-egg mayonnaise
1 tablespoon lemon juice
8 slices wholemeal bread

1 Combine turkey, celery, rocket,
almonds, sour cream, mayonnaise and
lemon juice in small bowl.
2 Spread turkey mixture over slices of
bread; top with the other slices.

GOAT'S CHEESE
& ROAST VEGGIE TART

**PREPARATION TIME 15 MINUTES *
COOKING TIME 20 MINUTES * SERVES 4**

1 ready-rolled butter
puff pastry sheet
2 cloves garlic, crushed
2 tablespoons fresh oregano leaves
3 cups (500g) coarsely chopped
roasted vegetables
1 medium plum tomato,
coarsely chopped
150g goat's cheese, crumbled

1 Preheat oven to very hot. Line oven tray with
baking parchment. Place pastry sheet on prepared
tray; spread with crushed garlic, sprinkle with
oregano.
2 Top with roasted vegetables, tomato and
goat's cheese.
3 Bake, uncovered, in very hot oven about
20 minutes or until pastry is browned lightly;
sprinkle with 1 tablespoon fresh oregano leaves.

CHRISTMAS CAKE CREAM PARFAITS

PREPARATION TIME 20 MINUTES *
SERVES 6

250g mascarpone
2 tablespoons whisky
1 tablespoon icing sugar
½ cup thickened cream
2 cups (300g) crumbled Christmas cake
2½ teaspoons whisky extra
raspberries and sifted icing sugar,
optional

1 Combine mascarpone, 2 tablespoons whisky and icing sugar in large bowl.
2 Beat cream in small bowl until soft peaks form; fold cream mixture into mascarpone mixture.
3 Layer 1 cup crumbled Christmas cake in base of six ¾-cup (180ml) glasses; sprinkle ½ teaspoon whisky over cake in each glass. Divide half of the mascarpone mixture among glasses.
4 Repeat process with another 1 cup crumbled Christmas cake, 2 teaspoons whisky and remaining mascarpone mixture. Cover; refrigerate until required.
5 Serve topped with raspberries and sifted icing sugar, if desired.

CHRISTMAS CAKE ICE-CREAM TERRINE

PREPARATION TIME 15 MINUTES (PLUS FREEZING TIME) *
SERVES 6

450g Christmas cake
2 tablespoons Cointreau
1 tablespoon finely grated orange rind
2 litres good-quality vanilla ice-cream, softened

1 Line 14cm x 21cm loaf tin with clingfilm. Cut Christmas cake into 1.5cm slices; brush cake slices with Cointreau.
2 Stir orange rind into ice-cream. Spread half of the ice-cream mixture into prepared tin; top with cake slices then remaining ice-cream. Cover with clingfilm; freeze until firm.
3 Using hot knife, cut terrine into six slices.

FRUIT CAKE 'N' EGGNOG CHEESECAKE

PREPARATION TIME 25 MINUTES (PLUS
COOLING AND REFRIGERATION TIME) *
COOKING TIME 55 MINUTES * SERVES 10

350g fruit cake, cut into
1cm slices
750g packaged cream
cheese, softened
300g sour cream
1 teaspoon vanilla extract
¼ cup (60ml) brandy
½ teaspoon ground nutmeg
2 cups (440g) caster sugar
3 eggs
1 cup (250ml) water
1 medium pink grapefruit
(425g), segmented
1 large orange (300g),
segmented
150g strawberries, halved
100g red seedless grapes
1 large kiwifruit (100g),
cut into 8 wedges

1 Preheat oven to moderate. Line base of 22cm springform tin with baking parchment.
2 Cover base of prepared tin with cake slices. Bake, uncovered, in moderate oven about 10 minutes or until browned lightly. Reduce oven temperature to slow.
3 Meanwhile, beat cream cheese, sour cream, extract, brandy, nutmeg and half of the sugar in medium bowl with electric mixer until smooth. Beat in eggs, one at a time, beat only until combined between each addition.
4 Pour mixture into tin. Bake, uncovered, in slow oven about 45 minutes or until just set. Cool cheesecake in oven with door ajar. Cover; refrigerate overnight.
5 Stir remaining sugar and the water in medium heavy-based frying pan over high heat until sugar dissolves; bring to a boil. Reduce heat; simmer, without stirring, uncovered, about 10 minutes or until toffee mixture is golden brown in colour. Remove from heat; stand until bubbles subside.
6 Meanwhile, remove cheesecake from tin, place on serving plate; top with fruit.
7 Working quickly, drizzle toffee over fruit.

COLD DESSERTS

FROSTED RASPBERRY CREAM MERINGUES

The meringues can be made three days ahead; store in an airtight container in a cool, dry place. In humid weather, make one day ahead.

8 large white muffin
paper cases
6 egg whites
pinch cream of tartar
1½ cups (330g) caster sugar
240g raspberries
1 egg white, beaten
lightly, extra
2 tablespoons white sugar
300ml thickened cream
2 tablespoons caster
sugar, extra
gold cachous

PREPARATION TIME 30 MINUTES (PLUS COOLING TIME)
❋ COOKING TIME 1 HOUR ❋ SERVES 8

1 Preheat oven to very slow (120°C/100°C fan-forced). Line two oven trays with slightly flattened paper cases (or trace four 8cm circles onto each of two sheets of baking parchment; turn paper marked side down onto oven trays).
2 Beat the six egg whites and cream of tartar in a medium bowl with an electric mixer until soft peaks form. Gradually add the 1½ cups caster sugar, beating until dissolved between additions.
3 Spoon meringue into a piping bag fitted with large fluted tube. Pipe meringue inside cases (or circles) to form a base; pipe around the edge to form sides.
4 Bake meringues for 1 hour or until dry and crisp; cool in oven with door ajar.
5 Meanwhile, brush half the raspberries individually with a little of the extra egg white. Toss raspberries in white sugar; place on tray lined with baking parchment. Allow to set for 1 hour or until sugar is dry.
6 Lightly crush the remaining raspberries in a bowl with a fork. Beat the cream and extra caster sugar in a small bowl with an electric mixer until soft peaks form; fold in crushed raspberries.
7 Just before serving, fill meringues with raspberry cream; top with frosted raspberries and cachous. Serve on white paper cases, if desired.

frosted raspberry
cream meringues

VERY-BERRY PAVLOVA

PREPARATION TIME 20 MINUTES * COOKING
TIME 25 MINUTES (PLUS COOLING AND
REFRIGERATION TIME) * SERVES 8

6 egg whites
1 cup (220g) caster sugar
1 tablespoon cornflour
600ml thickened cream
⅓ cup (75g) caster sugar, extra
300g fresh blueberries
360g fresh raspberries
250g strawberries, sliced thinly
2 tablespoons icing sugar

MIXED BERRY COULIS
120g fresh blueberries
120g fresh raspberries
120g fresh blackberries
¼ cup (55g) caster sugar

1 Preheat oven to moderate. Grease three oven trays, line with baking parchment; mark a 23cm-diameter circle on each piece of paper.
2 Beat egg whites in medium bowl with electric mixer until soft peaks form. Add sugar, 1 tablespoon at a time, beating until sugar dissolves between each addition; beat in cornflour.
3 Spread meringue over circles on prepared trays; bake, uncovered, in moderate oven 10 minutes. Reduce temperature to slow; bake 15 minutes. Cool meringues in oven with door ajar.
4 Meanwhile, make mixed berry coulis.
5 Beat cream and extra sugar in small bowl with electric mixer until firm peaks form.
6 Place one meringue on serving plate; flatten slightly. Layer with half of the cream mixture then top with half of the combined berries. Repeat layering with a second meringue, remaining cream and three-quarters of remaining berries, reserving remaining berries for garnish. Cover pavlova; refrigerate 3 hours.
7 Top pavlova with reserved berries, dust with sifted icing sugar; serve with coulis.

MIXED BERRY COULIS Combine ingredients in medium saucepan, simmer, uncovered, over low heat, about 10 minutes or until berries have softened. Push coulis mixture through sieve into medium bowl; cool. Discard seeds.

GLACÉ FRUIT SLICE WITH LIMONCELLO CREAM

An Italian lemon-flavoured liqueur, limoncello was originally made from the juice and peel of lemons grown along the coast of Amalfi. You can substitute it in this recipe, if you wish, with any lemon-flavoured liqueur or with an orange-flavoured one such as Cointreau. You will need approximately five lemons or oranges for this recipe.

PREPARATION TIME 30 MINUTES ∗ COOKING TIME 45 MINUTES (PLUS REFRIGERATION TIME)

90g butter, softened
1 tablespoon finely grated lemon rind
¾ cup (165g) caster sugar
2 eggs
¾ cup (110g) plain flour
½ cup (75g) self-raising flour
⅓ cup (80ml) milk
⅔ cup (150g) coarsely chopped glacé pineapple
⅔ cup (170g) coarsely chopped glacé apricots
⅔ cup (170g) coarsely chopped glacé peaches
¾ cup (110g) coarsely chopped dried pears
¾ cup (110g) toasted shelled pistachios

LEMON SYRUP
½ cup (125ml) lemon juice
1 cup (220g) caster sugar

LIMONCELLO CREAM
300ml thickened cream
2 tablespoons limoncello

1 Preheat oven to moderately slow. Line 20cm x 30cm shallow baking tin with baking parchment, extending paper 3cm over long sides.
2 Beat butter, rind and sugar in small bowl with electric mixer until light and fluffy. Add eggs, one at a time, beating well between additions. Mixture may curdle at this stage, but will come together later.
3 Transfer mixture to large bowl; stir in sifted flours, milk, fruit and nuts. Spread mixture into prepared tin. Bake, uncovered, in moderately slow oven about 45 minutes.
4 Meanwhile, make lemon syrup.
5 Remove slice from oven; pour hot syrup over hot slice in tin. Cover; refrigerate overnight.
6 Make limoncello cream.
7 Cut slice into small squares; serve with limoncello cream.

LEMON SYRUP Stir ingredients in small saucepan over heat, without boiling, until sugar dissolves; bring to a boil. Reduce heat; simmer, uncovered, without stirring, about 10 minutes or until thickened slightly.

LIMONCELLO CREAM Beat ingredients in small bowl with electric mixer until soft peaks form.

GOURMET CHOCOLATE TART

PREPARATION TIME 40 MINUTES (PLUS REFRIGERATION TIME) * COOKING TIME 30 MINUTES * SERVES 8

2 eggs
2 egg yolks
¼ cup (55g) caster sugar
250g dark eating chocolate, melted
200g butter, melted

TART SHELL
1½ cups (225g) plain flour
½ cup (110g) caster sugar
140g cold butter, chopped
1 egg, beaten lightly

1 Make tart shell, baking in moderately hot oven as instructed below then reducing oven temperature to moderate.
2 Whisk eggs, egg yolks and sugar in medium heatproof bowl over medium saucepan of simmering water about 15 minutes or until light and fluffy. Gently whisk chocolate and butter into egg mixture.
3 Pour mixture into shell. Bake, uncovered, in moderate oven about 10 minutes or until filling is set; cool 10 minutes. Refrigerate 1 hour. Serve dusted with cocoa powder, if desired.

TART SHELL Blend or process flour, sugar and butter until crumbly; add egg, process until ingredients just come together. Knead dough on floured surface until smooth. Enclose in clingfilm; refrigerate 30 minutes. Grease 24cm-round loose-base flan tin. Roll dough between sheets of baking parchment until large enough to line prepared tin. Lift dough onto tin; press into side, trim edge, prick base all over with fork. Cover; refrigerate 30 minutes. Preheat oven to moderately hot. Place tin on oven tray; cover dough with baking parchment, fill with dried beans or rice. Bake, uncovered, in moderately hot oven 10 minutes. Remove paper and beans carefully from tin; bake, uncovered, in moderately hot oven about 5 minutes or until tart shell browns lightly. Cool to room temperature.

EXOTIC FRUIT SALAD

You need about six medium passionfruit for this recipe.

PREPARATION TIME 20 MINUTES • COOKING TIME
15 MINUTES (PLUS COOLING AND REFRIGERATION TIME)
• SERVES 8

1 litre (4 cups) water
1 cup (270g) grated
palm sugar
1 vanilla pod
2cm piece fresh ginger
(10g), chopped finely
3 star anise
1 tablespoon finely grated
lime rind
⅓ cup (80ml) lime juice
½ cup coarsely chopped
fresh vietnamese mint
2 large mangoes (1.2kg),
chopped coarsely
3 star fruit (450g),
sliced thinly
2 large oranges (600g),
segmented
1 large pineapple (2kg),
chopped coarsely
1 medium papaya (1kg),
chopped coarsely
½ cup (125ml) passionfruit
pulp
12 rambutans (500g), halved
12 lychees (300g), halved

1 Stir the water and sugar in medium saucepan over high heat until sugar dissolves; bring to a boil. Reduce heat; simmer without stirring, uncovered, 5 minutes. Split vanilla bean in half lengthways; scrape seeds into pan. Add pod, ginger and star anise; simmer, uncovered, about 10 minutes or until syrup thickens. Discard pod; cool to room temperature. Stir in rind, juice and mint.
2 Combine remaining ingredients in large bowl. Pour syrup over fruit; stir gently to combine. Refrigerate fruit salad, covered, until cold.

FRUITY CHRISTMAS BOMBE
WITH BRANDY CREAM SAUCE

2 litres vanilla ice-cream, softened
⅓ cup (75g) chopped glacé pineapple
⅓ cup (85g) chopped glacé apricots
⅓ cup (70g) red glacé cherries, halved
¼ cup (50g) chopped glacé ginger
1 teaspoon mixed spice
1 teaspoon ground cinnamon
700g packet rich fruit cake

BRANDY CREAM SAUCE
300ml thickened cream
¼ cup (60ml) brandy
2 eggs, separated
½ cup (110g) caster sugar

PREPARATION TIME 20 MINUTES (PLUS FREEZING TIME)
∗ SERVES 8

1 Oil 1.75-litre (7-cup) pudding basin, line with clingfilm.
2 Combine ice-cream, fruit, ginger and spices in large bowl.
Spoon mixture into prepared basin, cover; freeze about
1 hour or until firm.
3 Split cake in half, cut halves to fit on top of ice-cream in
basin, press on gently. Cover; freeze overnight. Serve with
brandy cream sauce.

BRANDY CREAM SAUCE Beat cream and brandy in small bowl
with electric mixer until soft peaks form. Beat egg whites in
separate small bowl with electric mixer until soft peaks form,
gradually add sugar, beating well between additions. Add egg
yolks; beat well. Fold cream mixture into egg white mixture.

*fruity
christmas
bombe*

little frozen christmas puddings

LITTLE FROZEN CHRISTMAS PUDDINGS

PREPARATION TIME 20 MINUTES (PLUS FREEZING TIME)
∗ SERVES 8

2 cups (375g) mixed dried fruit
¼ cup (60g) chopped glacé peaches
¼ cup (60g) chopped glacé apricots
¼ cup (60ml) brandy
¾ cup (110g) macadamias, toasted,
chopped finely
1 teaspoon mixed spice
1 teaspoon ground cinnamon
2 litres good quality vanilla
ice-cream, softened
150g white eating chocolate, melted

1 Combine fruit and brandy in large bowl; cover, let stand overnight.
2 Line bases of eight 1-cup (250ml) freezer-proof moulds (we used tea cups) with baking parchment.
3 Stir nuts, spices and ice-cream into fruit mixture. Divide mixture among prepared moulds, cover; freeze overnight.
4 Turn puddings onto tray, peel away baking parchment. Spoon melted white chocolate into a small plastic bag, then snip off the corner of the bag. Drizzle the melted chocolate over the puddings.

FROZEN CHOCOLATE FRUIT CAKE PUDDING

PREPARATION TIME 40 MINUTES (PLUS STANDING, REFRIGERATION AND FREEZING TIME) * COOKING TIME 10 MINUTES

½ cup (95g) coarsely chopped dried figs
¼ cup (40g) coarsely chopped raisins
¼ cup (50g) coarsely chopped dried prunes
¼ cup (60g) coarsely chopped glacé cherries
4 fresh dates (100g), stoned, chopped coarsely
2 teaspoons finely grated orange rind
½ cup (125ml) brandy
125g butter
½ cup (75g) plain flour
½ cup (110g) firmly packed brown sugar
1 cup (250ml) milk
600ml thickened cream
⅔ cup (220g) chocolate hazelnut spread
1 teaspoon ground nutmeg
1 teaspoon ground cinnamon
4 egg yolks
⅓ cup (50g) toasted hazelnuts, chopped coarsely
200g dark eating chocolate, chopped finely
200g dark eating chocolate, melted, extra

1 Combine fruit, rind and brandy in large bowl; mix well. Cover tightly with clingfilm; store in a cool, dark place overnight or up to a week, stirring every day.

2 Line 17.5cm, 1.75-litre (7-cup) pudding basin with clingfilm, extending film 5cm over edge of basin.

3 Melt butter in medium saucepan, add flour; stir over heat until bubbling. Remove from heat; stir in sugar then milk and half of the cream. Stir over medium heat until mixture boils and thickens. Transfer to large bowl; stir in spread, spices and yolks. Cover surface of mixture with clingfilm; refrigerate 1 hour.

4 Stir in fruit mixture, nuts and chopped chocolate. Beat remaining cream in small bowl with electric mixer until soft peaks form, fold into pudding mixture. Spoon mixture into prepared basin, tap basin lightly to remove air bubbles. Cover with foil; freeze 3 hours or overnight.

5 Turn pudding onto tray; remove clingfilm, return pudding to freezer.

6 Cut a 35cm circle from a piece of paper to use as a guide; cover paper with clingfilm. Spread melted chocolate over clingfilm then quickly drape film, chocolate-side down, over pudding. Quickly smooth with hands, avoiding deep pleats in the film. Freeze until firm. Peel away film; trim away excess chocolate. Serve with a selection of fresh and frosted seasonal fruit, if desired.

Trio of sorbets

LEMON LIME

PREPARATION TIME
20 MINUTES * COOKING
TIME 10 MINUTES (PLUS
FREEZING TIME) * SERVES 8

2 tablespoons finely grated
lemon rind
1 tablespoon finely grated
lime rind
1 cup (220g) caster sugar
2½ cups (625ml) water
½ cup (125ml) lemon juice
¼ cup (60ml) lime juice
1 egg white

1 Stir rinds, sugar and the water
in medium saucepan over high
heat until sugar dissolves; bring
to a boil. Reduce heat; simmer
without stirring, uncovered,
5 minutes. Transfer to large
heatproof jug, cool to room
temperature; stir in juices.
2 Pour sorbet mixture into loaf
tin, cover tightly with foil; freeze
3 hours or overnight.
3 Process mixture with egg white
until smooth. Return to loaf tin,
cover; freeze until firm.

PASSIONFRUIT

*You need about 12 medium
passionfruit for this recipe.*

PREPARATION TIME
20 MINUTES * COOKING
TIME 10 MINUTES (PLUS
FREEZING TIME) * SERVES 8

1 cup (250ml) passionfruit pulp
1 cup (220g) caster sugar
2½ cups (625ml) water
¼ cup (60ml) lemon juice
2 egg whites

1 Strain pulp into small bowl.
Reserve seeds and juice.
2 Stir sugar and the water in
medium saucepan over high heat
until sugar dissolves; bring to
a boil. Reduce heat; simmer
without stirring, uncovered,
5 minutes. Transfer to large
heatproof jug, cool to room
temperature; stir in lemon juice
and passionfruit juice.
3 Pour sorbet mixture into loaf
tin, cover tightly with foil; freeze
3 hours or overnight.
4 Process mixture with egg
whites until smooth; stir in
reserved seeds. Return to loaf tin,
cover; freeze until firm.

RASPBERRY

PREPARATION TIME
20 MINUTES * COOKING
TIME 10 MINUTES (PLUS
FREEZING TIME) * SERVES 8

360g raspberries
1 cup (220g) caster sugar
2½ cups (625ml) water
1 tablespoon lemon juice
1 egg white

1 Press raspberries through sieve
into small bowl; discard seeds.
2 Stir sugar and the water in
medium saucepan over high heat
until sugar dissolves; bring to
a boil. Reduce heat; simmer
without stirring, uncovered,
5 minutes. Transfer to large
heatproof jug, cool to room
temperature; stir in raspberry
pulp and lemon juice.
3 Pour sorbet mixture into loaf
tin, cover tightly with foil;
freeze 3 hours or overnight.
4 Process mixture with egg white
until smooth. Return to loaf tin,
cover; freeze until firm.

CAKES & PUDDINGS

TRADITIONAL FRUIT CAKE

PREPARATION TIME 30 MINUTES *
COOKING TIME 3 HOURS * SERVES 36

2 cups (300g) currants
2 cups (340g) raisins, chopped coarsely
3 cups (500g) sultanas
½ cup (125ml) dark rum
150g butter
1 cup (200g) firmly packed brown sugar
4 eggs
½ cup (125ml) strawberry jam
1 cup (210g) glacé cherries, chopped coarsely
2 cups (340g) mixed peel
1 cup (140g) slivered almonds
2 cups (300g) plain flour
½ cup (75g) self-raising flour
½ teaspoon ground cinnamon
½ teaspoon ground allspice
blanched almonds and extra glacé cherries, to decorate
¼ cup (60ml) dark rum, extra

1 Combine dried fruit and rum in large bowl, cover; stand overnight.
2 Grease deep 23cm-round cake tin, line base and side with three layers baking parchment, extending paper 5cm above edge of tin.
3 Beat butter and sugar in small bowl with electric mixer until combined. Add eggs, one at a time, beating until just combined between additions; stir in jam. Stir into fruit mixture, then stir in cherries, peel, slivered almonds and sifted dry ingredients.
4 Spread cake mixture into prepared tin; decorate top with blanched almonds and extra glacé cherries, if desired. Bake in slow oven about 3 hours.
5 Brush top of hot cake with extra rum, cover tightly with foil; cool in tin.

traditional fruit cake

What you need to know...

Before you begin, quickly read this important information to guarantee your cake or pudding realises its full and delicious potential.

Lining cake tin

Smoothing mixture with spatula

Testing if cake is cooked

LINING CAKE TINS

To line the sides of a cake tin, cut three strips of baking parchment long enough to fit around the tin and 8cm wider than the depth of the tin. Fold strips lengthways about 2cm from edge and make diagonal cuts about 2cm apart up to the fold. Fit around the curves or corners of the tin, with cut section resting on the base. Using base of tin as a guide, cut three paper shapes to cover base of tin; place paper bases in position.

FILLING CAKE TIN

Spoon small amounts of cake mixture into corners of prepared tin, holding paper in position. Spread remaining mixture firmly into tin; smooth top with spatula or damp hand. Hold tin about 15cm above the worksurface; drop tin firmly onto worksurface to release air bubbles and settle mixture.

TO TEST IF CAKE IS COOKED

After minimum cooking time, feel top of cake with fingertips. If cake feels firm, gently push a sharp vegetable knife into the thickest part of the cake, as close to the centre as possible, right through to the base of tin. Gently withdraw knife and feel the blade; if the blade is simply sticky from fruit, the cake is cooked, but if there is moist cake mixture on the blade, return the cake to oven for a further 15 minutes before testing again.

WHEN CAKE IS COOKED

Make cuts in lining paper level with tin, fold down paper. Cover hot cake with foil, wrap in towel; cool in tin.

TO STORE CAKE

When cake has completely cooled, remove from tin. Leaving lining paper intact, wrap in clingfilm.
Place cake in airtight container or plastic freezer bag. Store in a cool place or freeze.

CAKE HINTS

The cake mixture can be made ahead – place cake mixture into prepared tin, cover the surface with clingfilm and refrigerate for 2 days. Stand mixture about 3 hours to return to room temperature before baking. Cold mixture will take about 30 minutes longer to cook.

TO STORE PUDDINGS

If pudding is calico-wrapped, hang pudding for 10 minutes after initial cooking. Remove cloth and allow to cool. Then, for all pudding recipes, wrap cooled pudding in clingfilm and seal in freezer bag or an airtight container; refrigerate or freeze.

REHEATING PUDDINGS

Three days before you want to use a frozen pudding, place it in the refrigerator to thaw. Remove pudding from refrigerator 12 hours before reheating.

TRADITIONAL STEAMED PUDDING: Remove clingfilm, return pudding to steamer and prepare as for cooking method. Steam for 2 hours.

TRADITIONAL BOILED PUDDING: Remove clingfilm and tie a clean, dry, unfloured cloth on pudding. Boil 2 hours as for cooking method. Hang hot pudding 10 minutes, remove cloth. Stand pudding 20 minutes for skin to darken.

PUDDING IN THE MICROWAVE: Reheat four single servings at once. Cover with clingfilm, microwave on HIGH (100%) for up to 1 minute per serving. To reheat whole pudding, cover with clingfilm, microwave on MEDIUM (50%) about 15 minutes or until hot.

Three-in-one christmas mix

One quantity of this basic fruit mixture recipe makes enough for three of these Christmas recipes – the cake, the pudding (page 108) and the fruit slice (page 110). The mixture can be made a month before required, and stored in a cool, dark place – your refrigerator is ideal. Ideally, the ingredients shown below as 'chopped' should all be cut to a similar size, about that of a sultana. Grand Marnier liqueur was used in keeping with the citrus content of the mixture (you can use any citrus-flavoured liqueur), but it can be substituted with rum, sherry or brandy.

BASIC FRUIT MIXTURE

PREPARATION TIME 45 MINUTES
(PLUS STANDING TIME)

6 cups (1kg) sultanas
2½ cups (375g) dried currants
2¼ cups (425g) raisins, chopped
1½ cups (250g) stoned dried dates, chopped
1½ cups (250g) stoned prunes, chopped
1¼ cups (250g) glacé cherries, quartered
½ cup (125g) glacé apricots, chopped
½ cup (115g) glacé pineapple, chopped
½ cup (115g) glacé ginger, chopped
¼ cup (120g) mixed peel
3 medium apples (450g), peeled, grated
⅔ cup (240g) fig jam
2 tablespoons finely grated orange rind
¼ cup (60ml) lemon juice
2 cups (440g) firmly packed brown sugar
1 tablespoon mixed spice
1⅓ cups (330ml) Grand Marnier

1 Mix ingredients in large bowl; cover tightly with clingfilm. Store mixture in cool, dark place for a month (or longer, if desired) before using; stir mixture every two or three days.

MOIST CHRISTMAS CAKE

PREPARATION TIME 15 MINUTES
• COOKING TIME 3 HOURS (PLUS COOLING TIME)

½ quantity basic fruit mixture
250g butter, melted, cooled
5 eggs, beaten lightly
2½ cups (375g) plain flour
2 tablespoons Grand Marnier

1 Preheat oven to slow. Line base and sides of deep 22cm-square cake tin with one thickness brown paper and two thicknesses baking parchment, extending papers 5cm above sides of tin.
2 Place basic fruit mixture in large bowl. Mix in butter and eggs then sifted flour in two batches.
3 Spread mixture into prepared tin; level top with spatula. Bake, uncovered, in slow oven about 3 hours. Brush with liqueur; cover hot cake in tin with foil, cool overnight.

TIP Can be made three months ahead and stored in an airtight container under refrigeration.

CHRISTMAS PUDDING

PREPARATION TIME 15 MINUTES * COOKING TIME
4 HOURS (PLUS STANDING TIME)

You need a 60cm square of unbleached calico for the pudding cloth. If calico has not been used before, soak overnight in cold water; next day, boil it for 20 minutes then rinse in cold water.

¼ quantity basic fruit mixture
(see page 106)
250g butter, melted, cooled
3 eggs, beaten lightly
4 cups (280g) stale breadcrumbs
¼ cup (35g) plain flour

1 Place basic fruit mixture in large bowl. Mix in butter and eggs then breadcrumbs and the flour.

2 Fill large boiler three-quarters full of hot water, cover; bring to a boil. Have ready 2.5 metres of kitchen string and an extra ½ cup of plain flour. Wearing thick rubber gloves, put pudding cloth in boiling water; boil 1 minute; squeeze excess water from cloth. Working quickly, spread hot cloth on bench, rub flour into centre of cloth to cover an area about 40cm in diameter, leaving flour a little thicker in centre of cloth where 'skin' on the pudding needs to be thickest.

3 Place pudding mixture in centre of cloth. Gather cloth evenly around mixture, avoiding any deep pleats; then pat into round shape. Tie cloth tightly with string as close to mixture as possible. Pull ends of cloth tightly to ensure pudding is as round and firm as possible. Knot two pairs of corners together to make pudding easier to remove.

4 Lower pudding into boiling water; tie free ends of string to handles of boiler to suspend pudding. Cover with tight-fitting lid; boil rapidly for 4 hours, replenishing water as necessary to maintain level.

5 Untie pudding from handles; place wooden spoon through knotted calico loops to lift pudding from water. Do not put pudding on bench; suspend from spoon by placing over rungs of upturned stool or wedging handle in a drawer. Pudding must be suspended freely. Twist wet ends of cloth around string to avoid them touching pudding. If pudding has been cooked correctly, cloth will start to dry in patches within a few minutes; hang 10 minutes.

6 Place pudding on board; cut string, carefully peel back cloth. Turn pudding onto a plate then carefully peel cloth away completely; cool. Stand at least 20 minutes or until skin darkens and pudding becomes firm.

TIP For tips on how to store and reheat your pudding, see page 105.

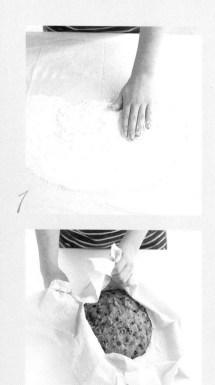

1 Rub about a 40-cm area of flour onto damp hot cloth, leaving flour a little thicker in the centre.

2 Gather cloth evenly around the pudding mixture, avoiding any deep pleats; pat into round shape.

3 Lower pudding into boiling water; tie string ends to handles of the boiler to suspend the pudding.

4 Place a wooden spoon through the knotted loops of the cloth to lift pudding from boiling water.

FRUIT
MINCE SLICE

**PREPARATION TIME
10 MINUTES ∗ COOKING
TIME 25 MINUTES**

2 sheets ready-rolled
puff pastry
¼ quantity basic fruit
mixture (see page 106)
1 egg white, beaten lightly
1 tablespoon caster sugar

1 Preheat oven to hot.
Grease 20cm x 30cm
shallow baking tin.
2 Cut one pastry sheet large
enough to cover base of prepared tin. Using fork, prick
pastry all over several times.
Place 19cm x 29cm baking
tray on top of pastry to prevent it rising during cooking.
3 Bake pastry in hot oven
about 10 minutes or until
pastry is browned lightly
and crisp.
4 Remove baking tray;
spread fruit mixture evenly
over cooked pastry.
5 Cut remaining pastry
sheet large enough to cover
fruit mixture. Brush pastry
with egg white, sprinkle
with sugar; carefully score
pastry in crosshatch pattern.
Bake, uncovered, in hot oven
about 15 minutes or until
pastry is browned. Serve
slice with custard, if desired

BEST-EVER BOILED FRUIT CAKE

PREPARATION TIME 30 MINUTES * COOKING TIME
2 HOURS 45 MINUTES * SERVES 36

2⅓ cups (375g) sultanas
2¼ cups (375g) chopped
raisins
¾ cup (110g) dried currants
½ cup (105g) glacé
cherries, halved
250g butter, chopped
coarsely
1 cup (200g) firmly packed
brown sugar
½ cup (125ml) sweet sherry
¼ cup (60ml) water
1 tablespoon treacle
2 teaspoons finely grated
orange rind
2 teaspoons finely
lemon rind
5 eggs, beaten lightly
1¾ cups (260g) plain flour
⅓ cup (50g) self-raising flour
extra glacé cherries,
to decorate

1 Combine fruit, butter, sugar, sherry and the water in large saucepan. Stir over heat, without boiling, until butter melts and sugar dissolves. Bring to a boil, then remove from heat. Transfer mixture to large heatproof bowl; cool.
2 Grease deep 19cm-square cake tin or deep 23cm-round cake tin, line base and sides with three layers baking parchment, extending paper 5cm above edge of tin.
3 Stir treacle, rinds and egg into fruit mixture, then stir in flours. Spread cake mixture into prepared tin; decorate top with extra glacé cherries, if desired. Bake in slow oven about 2¾ hours. Cover hot cake tightly with foil; cool in tin.

LAST-MINUTE FRUIT CAKE

PREPARATION TIME 20 MINUTES • COOKING
TIME 2 HOURS (PLUS COOLING TIME)

1½ cups (240g) sultanas
1 cup (170g) raisins, chopped coarsely
1 cup (150g) currants
½ cup (85g) mixed peel
⅓ cup (70g) glacé cherries, halved
2 tablespoons coarsely chopped
glacé pineapple
2 tablespoons coarsely chopped
glacé apricots
185g butter, chopped
¾ cup (165g) firmly packed
brown sugar
⅓ cup (80ml) brandy
⅓ cup (80ml) water
2 teaspoons finely grated orange rind
1 teaspoon finely grated lemon rind
1 tablespoon treacle
3 eggs, beaten lightly
1¼ cups (185g) plain flour
¼ cup (35g) self-raising flour
½ teaspoon bicarbonate of soda
½ cup (80g) blanched almonds

1 Line deep 20cm-round cake tin with three
thicknesses of baking parchment, extending paper
5cm above side.
2 Combine fruit, butter, sugar, brandy and the
water in medium saucepan, stir over medium heat
until butter is melted and sugar is dissolved; bring
to the boil. Remove from heat; transfer to large
bowl. Cool to room temperature.
3 Preheat oven to slow.
4 Stir rinds, treacle and eggs into fruit mixture
then sifted dry ingredients. Spread mixture into
prepared tin; decorate with nuts.
5 Bake in slow oven, uncovered, about 2 hours.
Cover hot cake with foil; cool in tin overnight.

microwave puddings

MICROWAVE PUDDINGS

We used a 600-watt micro-wave oven for this recipe.

2¾ cups (500g) mixed
dried fruit
⅓ cup (80ml) brandy
125g butter
¾ cup (150g) firmly packed
dark brown sugar
2 tablespoons golden syrup
2 eggs
1 large (200g) apple, peeled,
grated coarsely
¾ cup (110g) plain flour
2 teaspoons mixed spice
½ teaspoon bicarbonate
of soda

PREPARATION TIME 20 MINUTES *
COOKING TIME 19 MINUTES * MAKES 8

1 Grease eight ¾-cup (180ml) microwave-safe dishes.
2 Combine fruit and brandy in another small microwave-safe bowl; cook, covered, on HIGH (100%) 1 minute.
3 Beat butter, sugar and syrup in small bowl with electric mixer until combined. Add eggs, one at a time, beating until just combined between additions. Transfer mixture to large bowl; stir in fruit mixture, apple and sifted dry ingredients.
4 Divide mixture evenly among prepared dishes, smooth tops.
5 Arrange dishes around edge of microwave turntable; cook, uncovered, on MEDIUM (50%) 10 minutes. Rotate dishes; cook on MEDIUM (50%) further 8 minutes or until centres of puddings are almost set. Stand puddings 10 minutes; centres of puddings should be firm. Turn puddings onto serving dishes.

ALLERGY-FREE PUDDING

This recipe is gluten-free, contains no dairy products or eggs, and makes one cake or pudding

2¼ cups (360g) sultanas
1½ cups (250g) chopped raisins
½ cup (75g) dried currants
1½ cups (250g) chopped stoned dates
1½ cups (375ml) water
½ cup (125ml) orange juice
2 tablespoons honey
1 cup (200g) firmly packed brown sugar
185g dairy-free margarine
1 cup (125g) soy flour
1 cup (150g) rice flour
1 teaspoon cream of tartar
½ teaspoon bicarbonate of soda
2 teaspoons mixed spice
1 cup (125g) ground almonds

PREPARATION TIME 20 MINUTES *
COOKING TIME 6 HOURS * **SERVES 10**

1 Combine fruit, the water, juice, honey, sugar and margarine in large saucepan. Stir over heat, without boiling, until margarine melts. Transfer mixture to large heatproof bowl; cool.
2 Grease 2.25-litre (9-cup) pudding basin, line base with baking parchment.
3 Stir sifted dry ingredients and ground almonds into fruit mixture. Spoon mixture into prepared basin, cover pudding with greased foil; secure with lid or kitchen string. Place basin in large saucepan with enough boiling water to come halfway up side of basin; simmer, covered, about 6 hours, adding more boiling water as necessary.

CAKE

PREPARATION TIME 20 MINUTES * **COOKING TIME 2 HOURS 30 MINUTES** * **SERVES 10**

1 Grease a deep 19cm-square cake tin, line base and sides with three layers baking parchment, extending paper 5cm above edge of tin.
2 Complete cake mixture following instructions above, then spread mixture into prepared tin; bake in slow oven about 2½ hours, covering loosely with foil after 1 hour. Cover hot cake tightly with foil; cool in tin.

Four quick toppings for puddings

These Christmas pudding accompaniments are so delectable you might have to make all four! The recipes for butters will freeze successfully for up to 4 weeks, covered tightly. The other recipes are best made just before serving.

CINNAMON RUM BUTTER

SERVES 12

250g soft butter
1 cup (200g) firmly packed brown sugar
2 teaspoons ground cinnamon
2 tablespoons dark rum

Beat butter, sugar and cinnamon in small bowl with electric mixer until light and fluffy; add rum, beat until combined. Spoon mixture into piping bag fitted with medium fluted tube. Pipe mixture into twelve 5cm rounds on clingfilm-lined tray. Refrigerate until firm.

ORANGE LIQUEUR BUTTER

SERVES 6

125g soft butter
2 teaspoons finely grated orange rind
½ cup (80g) icing sugar
2 tablespoons Irish cream liqueur

Beat butter and rind in small bowl with electric mixer until light and fluffy; gradually add sifted icing sugar, beat until smooth. Add liqueur, beat until combined. Spoon mixture into serving bowl.

EASY COFFEE SAUCE

SERVES 8

1 litre vanilla ice-cream
2 tablespoons dry instant coffee
1 tablespoon boiling water

Stand ice-cream at room temperature until melted. Dissolve coffee and boiling water in small bowl; stir into melted ice-cream.

CARAMEL RUM CUSTARD

SERVES 6

600ml carton prepared vanilla custard
1 tablespoon dark rum
¾ cup (150g) firmly packed brown sugar
2 teaspoons vanilla essence

Combine custard, rum and sugar in medium saucepan; stir over low heat until sugar is dissolved. Stir in essence. Serve warm or cold.

GINGERBREAD HOUSE

PREPARATION TIME 2 HOURS 30 MINUTES (PLUS REFRIGERATION TIME) · COOKING TIME 45 MINUTES (PLUS STANDING TIME)

You need thin cardboard or thick paper to make patterns for the house. The house can be assembled three days ahead.

4½ cups (675g) self-raising flour
3 teaspoons ground ginger
2 teaspoons ground cinnamon
1½ teaspoons ground cloves
1 teaspoon ground nutmeg
185g butter, chopped
1 cup (220g) firmly packed dark brown sugar
½ cup (180g) treacle
2 eggs, beaten lightly
35cm round or square cake board
assorted lollies

ROYAL ICING
2 egg whites
3 cups (480g) pure icing sugar

1 Process flour, spices and butter until mixture is crumbly (you may have to process in two batches). Add sugar, treacle and enough egg for mixture to just combine. Turn dough onto floured surface; knead until smooth. Cover; refrigerate 1 hour.

2 Meanwhile, cut paper patterns for gingerbread house: cut two 12cm x 19cm rectangles for roof; two 10.5cm x 16cm rectangles for side walls of house; and two 16cm x 18cm rectangles for front and back walls of house. Trim front and back walls to form two 11cm-high gables.

3 Preheat oven to moderate. Roll dough between sheets of baking parchment until 5mm thick. Peel away top layer of paper; use patterns to cut shapes from dough. Pull away excess dough; slide baking parchment with shapes onto oven tray; bake, uncovered, in moderate oven about 12 minutes or until shapes are just firm (they become crisp after they cool). Re-roll dough scraps into one 5mm-thick piece; cut out trees and chimney.

4 While shapes are still warm and soft, use tip of sharp knife to cut out small windows from side walls of house, then cut out door from front wall; reserve cut-out door piece. Trim shapes to straighten sides; transfer all shapes to wire racks to cool.

5 Make royal icing. Cover board with foil or silver paper.

6 Secure two crossed skewers to back of each roof piece with icing. Allow to dry before assembling house.

7 Assemble house, securing roof and walls together with icing. If possible, stand house several hours or overnight, supporting sides with four cans, so that it is thoroughly dry before decorating. Decorate board around house with remaining icing to resemble fallen snow.

8 Secure door to house with icing; decorate house with lollies, securing with icing. Secure trees to board and chimney to roof with icing. Dust house with a little sifted icing sugar, if desired.

ROYAL ICING Beat egg whites in small bowl with electric mixer until frothy; gradually beat in sifted icing sugar. Cover icing with damp cloth while not using.

TIPS You can fill the house with sweets before putting on the roof. We used mint leaves, bullets, M&M's, mini M&M's, rainbow drops, chocolate-covered sultanas and chocolate buttons for our gingerbread house.

CHRISTMAS NUT TREE

PREPARATION TIME 30 MINUTES (PLUS REFRIGERATION TIME)

Bring out this tree with the coffee, suggesting to your guests that they snap off bits of the branches. Or, for an impressive gift, wrap the whole tree in cellophane and deliver it on the day.

24cm-round covered cake board
500g dark eating chocolate, melted
1 cup (140g) toasted slivered almonds, chopped finely
½ cup (95g) finely chopped dried figs
100g dark eating chocolate, melted, extra
1 brazil nut
2 teaspoons icing sugar

1 Grease four oven trays; line each with baking parchment. Mark nine crosses, measuring 7cm, 9cm, 11cm, 13cm, 14cm, 15cm, 16cm, 17cm and 18cm on trays, leaving about 3cm space between each cross. Mark an 18cm cross on cake board.
2 Combine chocolate, almonds and figs in medium bowl. Drop teaspoonfuls of the chocolate mixture along all the marked crosses to make branches; refrigerate several hours or overnight.
3 Drop about a teaspoon of the extra melted chocolate into the centre of the 18cm cross on cake board; position the 18cm branch on top, moving it around until the best position is found.
4 Assemble the remaining eight branches in pairs, starting from the largest remaining branch and finishing with the smallest, using about a teaspoon of the extra melted chocolate in the centre of each crossed pair; refrigerate until set.
5 Secure each pair to the next with a little melted chocolate (if the branches look a little uneven, support them underneath with a match box). Secure brazil nut to centre of smallest branch with remaining melted chocolate; refrigerate until chocolate sets between branches. Store tree in refrigerator until required; dust with sifted icing sugar.

Mark nine crosses on trays, leaving about 3cm space between each cross.

Mark nine crosses on trays, leaving about 3cm space between each cross.

Assemble branches in pairs, securing one pair to the next with melted chocolate.

Truffles

CRANBERRY, PORT & DARK CHOCOLATE

PREPARATION TIME 40 MINUTES (PLUS REFRIGERATION TIME) * COOKING TIME 5 MINUTES * MAKES 30

¼ cup (60ml) thickened cream
200g dark eating chocolate, chopped coarsely
2 tablespoons port
⅓ cup (50g) dried cranberries, chopped coarsely
300g dark eating chocolate, melted

1 Combine cream and chopped chocolate in small saucepan; stir over low heat until smooth, stir in port and cranberries. Transfer to small bowl, cover; refrigerate 3 hours or overnight.
2 Working with a quarter of the chocolate mixture at a time (keeping remainder under refrigeration), roll rounded teaspoons into balls; place on tray. Freeze truffles until firm.
3 Working quickly, dip truffles in melted chocolate then roll gently in hands to coat evenly, return to tray; refrigerate until firm.

WHITE CHOC, LEMON, LIME & COCONUT

PREPARATION TIME 40 MINUTES (PLUS REFRIGERATION TIME) * COOKING TIME 5 MINUTES * MAKES 30

½ cup (125ml) coconut cream
2 teaspoons finely grated lime rind
2 teaspoons finely grated lemon rind
360g white eating chocolate, chopped coarsely
1¼ cups (85g) shredded coconut

1 Combine coconut cream, rinds and chocolate in small saucepan; stir over low heat until smooth. Transfer mixture to small bowl, cover; refrigerate 3 hours or overnight.
2 Working with a quarter of the chocolate mixture at a time (keeping remainder under refrigeration), roll rounded teaspoons into balls; place on tray. Refrigerate truffles until firm.
3 Working quickly, roll truffles in coconut, return to tray; refrigerate until firm.

PEANUT BUTTER
& MILK CHOCOLATE

PREPARATION TIME 40 MINUTES (PLUS
REFRIGERATION TIME) · COOKING TIME
5 MINUTES · MAKES 30

⅓ cup (80ml) thickened cream
200g milk eating chocolate, chopped coarsely
¼ cup (70g) unsalted crunchy peanut butter
¾ cup (110g) crushed peanuts

1 Combine cream and chocolate in small saucepan;
stir over low heat until smooth, stir in peanut
butter. Transfer to small bowl, cover; refrigerate
3 hours or overnight.
2 Working with a quarter of the chocolate mixture
at a time (keeping remainder under refrigeration),
roll rounded teaspoons into balls; place on tray.
Refrigerate truffles until firm.
3 Working quickly, roll balls in peanuts, return to
tray; refrigerate truffles until firm.

DARK CHOCOLATE
& GINGER

PREPARATION TIME 40 MINUTES (PLUS
REFRIGERATION TIME) · COOKING TIME
5 MINUTES · MAKES 30

⅓ cup (80ml) thickened cream
200g dark eating chocolate, chopped coarsely
½ cup (115g) glacé ginger, chopped finely
¼ cup (25g) cocoa powder

1 Combine cream and chocolate in small saucepan; stir over low heat until smooth, stir in ginger.
Transfer to small bowl, cover; refrigerate 3 hours or
overnight.
2 Working with a quarter of the chocolate mixture
at a time (keeping remainder under refrigeration),
roll rounded teaspoons into balls; place on tray.
Refrigerate truffles until firm.
3 Working quickly, roll balls in cocoa, return to
tray; refrigerate truffles until firm.

Conversion charts

MEASURES

The cup and spoon measurements used in this book are metric: one measuring cup holds approximately 250ml; one metric tablespoon holds 20ml; one metric teaspoon holds 5ml. All cup and spoon measurements are level.

The most accurate way of measuring dry ingredients is to weigh them. When measuring liquids, use a clear glass or plastic jug with metric markings.

We use large eggs with an average weight of 60g.

WARNING This book contains recipes for dishes made with raw or lightly cooked eggs. These should be avoided by vulnerable people such as pregnant and nursing mothers, invalids, the elderly, babies and young children.

OVEN TEMPERATURES

These oven temperatures are only a guide for conventional ovens. For fan-assisted ovens, check the manufacturer's manual.

	°C (Celcius)	°F (Fahrenheit)	gas mark
Very low	120	250	½
Low	150	275–300	1–2
Moderately low	170	325	3
Moderate	180	350–375	4–5
Moderately hot	200	400	6
Hot	220	425–450	7–8
Very hot	240	475	9

DRY MEASURES

metric	imperial
15g	½oz
30g	1oz
60g	2oz
90g	3oz
125g	4oz (¼lb)
155g	5oz
185g	6oz
220g	7oz
250g	8oz (½lb)
280g	9oz
315g	10oz
345g	11oz
375g	12oz (¾lb)
410g	13oz
440g	14oz
470g	15oz
500g	16oz (1lb)
750g	24oz (1½lb)
1kg	32oz (2lb)

LIQUID MEASURES

metric	imperial
30ml	1 fl oz
60ml	2 fl oz
100ml	3 fl oz
125ml	4 fl oz
150ml	5 fl oz (¼ pt/1 gill)
190ml	6 fl oz
250ml	8 fl oz
300ml	10 fl oz (½ pt)
500ml	16 fl oz
600ml	20 fl oz (1 pt)
1000ml (1 litre)	1¾ pts

LENGTH MEASURES

metric	imperial
3mm	⅛in
6mm	¼in
1cm	½in
2cm	¾in
2.5cm	1in
5cm	2in
6cm	2½in
8cm	3in
10cm	4in
13cm	5in
15cm	6in
18cm	7in
20cm	8in
23cm	9in
25cm	10in
28cm	11in
30cm	12in (1ft)

Index

Allergy-free pudding 116
Apple sauce 30, 45
Asian-spiced turkey with cran-
  berry & peach chutney 25
Asian-style baked ham 42
Asparagus, pan-fried with
  Parmesan 9

Baby beetroot with caper
  vinaigrette 72
Baby carrots with orange
  maple syrup 65
Balsamic dressing 56, 74
Balsamic-glazed baby onions
  61
Barbecued corn, broad beans
  & peppers 69
Basic fruit mixture 106
Basil oil 10
beans
  Barbecued corn, broad
  beans & peppers 69
  Peas & beans with hazelnuts
  66
beef
  Herbed beef fillet with
  horseradish cream sauce
  33
  Spiced beef with chilli jam 34
beetroot
  Baby beetroot with caper
  vinaigrette 72
  Roasted beetroot & onion
  73
Best-ever boiled fruit cake 111
Blood orange marmalade
  glazed ham 41
Boned shoulder of lamb with
  coriander hazelnut pesto 38
Boned turkey breast with
  couscous stuffing 20
Brandy cream sauce 96
Broccolini polonaise 62
butters
  Cinnamon rum butter 118
  Orange liqueur butter 118

Caper vinaigrette 72
Caramel rum custard 118

Carrots with orange maple
  syrup 65
Celeriac, roasted garlic 59
Chargrilled poultry platter
  with lemon dressing 26
cheese
  Goat's cheese & roast veggie
  tart 83
  Pan-fried asparagus with
  Parmesan 9
  Peas with caraway &
  Parmesan 65
  Roasted vegetable & goat's
  cheese terrine 10
Cheesecake, fruit cake 'n'
  eggnog 86
Chilli jam 34
chocolate
  Christmas nut tree 122
  Cranberry, port & dark
  chocolate truffles 124
  Dark chocolate & ginger
  truffles 125
  Frozen chocolate fruit cake
  pudding 98
  Gourmet chocolate tart 94
  Peanut butter & milk
  chocolate truffles 125
  White choc, lemon, lime &
  coconut truffles 124
Christmas cake
  cream parfaits 85
  ice-cream terrine 85
  see also fruit cakes
Christmas nut tree 122
Christmas pudding 108
  Allergy-free 116
  Basic fruit mixture 106
  Little frozen Christmas
  puddings 97
  Microwave puddings 115
  reheating 105
  storing 105
Cinnamon rum butter 118
Coffee sauce 118
Corn, barbecued, broad beans
  & peppers 69
Coulis, mixed berry 91
couscous

Boned turkey breast with
  couscous stuffing 20
Middle-eastern lamb with
  olive couscous stuffing 37
cranberry
  Cranberry & peach
  chutney 25
  Cranberry, port & dark
  chocolate truffles 124
Dark chocolate & ginger
  truffles 125
Devilled sauce 44
dressings
  Balsamic 56, 74
  Caper vinaigrette 72
  Lemon 26
  Port & basil 71
  Raspberry vinaigrette 61
duck
  Chargrilled poultry platter
  with lemon dressing 26
  Garlic roasted duck 15

Easy coffee sauce 118
Egg & ham slice 79
Exotic fruit salad 95

Fig & orange glazed ham 39
Forcemeat stuffing 14
Frosted raspberry cream
  meringues 88
Frozen chocolate fruit cake
  pudding 98
Fruit cake 'n' eggnog cheese-
  cake 86
fruit cakes
  Allergy-free 116
  Basic fruit mixture 106
  Best-ever boiled 111
  filling cake tins 104
  hints 105
  Last-minute 112
  lining cake tins 104
  Moist Christmas cake 106
  storing 105
  testing if a cake is cooked 104
  Traditional 102
Fruit mince slice 110

Fruit salad, exotic 95
Fruity Christmas bombe with
  brandy cream sauce 96

Garlic & rosemary roasted
  vegetables 58
Garlic roasted duck 15
Gingerbread house 121
Glacé fruit slice with
  Limoncello cream 92
Goat's cheese & roast veggie
  tart 83
Gourmet chocolate tart 94
Gravy 16, 44
  Port gravy 18

ham
  Asian-style baked 42
  Blood orange marmalade
  glazed 41
  Fig & orange glazed 39
  Ham & egg slice 79
Hazelnuts, peas & beans
  with 66
Herbed beef fillet with horse-
  radish cream sauce 33
Honey-glazed pork with sage
  28
Horseradish cream sauce 33

ice-cream
  Christmas cake ice-cream
  terrine 85
  Frozen chocolate fruit cake
  pudding 98
  Fruity Christmas bombe
  with brandy cream sauce 96
  Lemon lime sorbet 101
  Little frozen Christmas
  puddings 97
  Passionfruit sorbet 101
  Raspberry sorbet 101

lamb
  Boned shoulder of lamb
  with coriander hazelnut
  pesto 38
  Middle-eastern lamb with
  olive couscous stuffing 37

Last-minute fruit cake 112
Leeks in vinaigrette 61
lemon
    Glacé fruit slice with
      Limoncello cream 92
    Lemon dressing 26
    Lemon lime sorbet 101
    Lemon parsley stuffing 16
    White choc, lemon, lime &
      coconut truffles 124
lime
    Lemon lime sorbet 101
    White choc, lemon, lime &
      coconut truffles 124
Limoncello cream 92
Little frozen Christmas
    puddings 97

meat, roasting 12
Mediterranean potato mash
    56
Meringues, frosted raspberry
    cream 88
Microwave puddings 115
Middle-eastern lamb with olive
    couscous stuffing 37
Mint sauce, traditional 45
Moist Christmas cake 106
Mushrooms, roasted 71
Mustard & honey-glazed
    roasted sweet potatoes 57

Olive couscous stuffing 37
onions
    Balsamic-glazed baby
      onions 61
    Roasted beetroot & onion
      73
Orange liqueur butter 118

Pan-fried asparagus with
    Parmesan 9
Passionfruit sorbet 101
Pavlova, very-berry 91
Peanut butter & milk choco-
    late truffles 125
peas
    Peas & beans with hazelnuts
      66
    Peas with caraway &
      Parmesan 65
    Salmon, pea & mint
      linguine 80
    Sesame patty-pan squash
      & sugar snap peas 69

peppers
    Barbecued corn, broad
      beans & peppers 69
    Roasted peppers with port
      & basil dressing 71
    Roasted vegetable &
      goat's cheese terrine 10
Perfect roast potatoes 55
Pomegranate-glazed turkey
    with cornbread stuffing 23
pork
    Asian-style baked ham 42
    Blood orange marmalade
      glazed ham 41
    Fig & orange glazed ham 39
    Honey-glazed pork with
      sage 28
    Rack of pork with apple
      sauce 30
Port & basil dressing 71
Port gravy 18
potatoes
    Garlic & rosemary roasted
      vegetables 58
    Mediterranean potato mash
      56
    Perfect roast potatoes 55
    Traditional roast potatoes
      54
    Warm potato salad with
      caperberries 52
poultry
    roasting 12
    testing if poultry is cooked
      14
Prawns, slow-cooked spicy
    herbed 4

Rack of pork with apple sauce
    30
raspberry
    Frosted raspberry cream
      meringues 88
    Raspberry sorbet 101
    Raspberry vinaigrette 61
    Very-berry Pavlova 91
Roasted beetroot & onion 73
Roasted garlic celeriac 59
Roasted mushrooms 71
Roasted peppers with port &
    basil dressing 71
Roasted tomatoes with
    balsamic dressing 74
Roasted vegetable & goat's
    cheese terrine 10

Roasted vine tomatoes with
    crispy basil leaves 75
roasts 12
Royal icing 121

salmon
    Salmon, pea & mint
      linguine 80
    Slow-roasted pesto 51
    Slow-roasted 48
    Smoked salmon & dilled
      sour cream crepe cakes 7
Salt-crusted ocean trout with
    Thai-flavours hollandaise 46
sauces
    Brandy cream sauce 96
    Caramel rum custard 118
    Devilled sauce 44
    Easy coffee sauce 118
    Gravy 16, 44
    Horseradish cream 33
    Port gravy 18
    Thai-flavours hollandaise 46
    Traditional mint sauce 45
Sausagemeat stuffing 18
Sesame patty-pan squash &
    sugar snap peas 69
Slow-cooked spicy herbed
    prawns 4
Slow-roasted pesto salmon 51
Slow-roasted salmon 48
Slow-roasted turkey with
    sausagemeat stuffing &
    port gravy 18
Smoked salmon & dilled sour
    cream crepe cakes 7
sorbets
    Lemon lime 101
    Passionfruit 101
    Raspberry 101
Spiced beef with chilli jam 34
Spinach & squash frittata 9
squash
    Sesame patty-pan squash
      & sugar snap peas 69
    Squash & spinach frittata 9
stuffings
    Cornbread 23
    Couscous 20
    Forcemeat 14
    Lemon parsley 16
    Olive couscous 37
    Sausagemeat 18
Sugar snap peas, sesame
    patty-pan squash & 69

Sweet potatoes, mustard &
    honey-glazed roasted 57

Thai-flavours hollandaise 46
Three-in-one Christmas mix
    106
tomatoes
    Roasted tomatoes with
      balsamic dressing 74
    Roasted vine tomatoes with
      crispy basil leaves 75
Traditional fruit cake 102
Traditional mint sauce 45
Traditional roast potatoes 54
Traditional turkey with
    forcemeat stuffing 14
Trout, salt-crusted with Thai-
    flavours hollandaise 46
truffles
    Cranberry, port & dark
      chocolate 124
    Dark chocolate & ginger
      125
    Peanut butter & milk
      chocolate 125
    White choc, lemon, lime
      & coconut 124
turkey
    Asian-spiced turkey with
      cranberry & peach
      chutney 25
    Boned turkey breast with
      couscous stuffing 20
    Pomegranate-glazed turkey
      with cornbread stuffing 23
    Slow-roasted turkey with
      sausagemeat stuffing &
      port gravy 18
    Traditional turkey with
      forcemeat stuffing 14
    Turkey rillettes 76
    Turkey salad sandwiches 83
    Turkey with lemon parsley
      stuffing 16
    Vietnamese turkey salad 78

Vegetables, garlic & rosemary
    roasted 58
Very-berry Pavlova 91
Vietnamese turkey salad 78

Warm potato salad with
    caperberries 52
White choc, lemon, lime &
    coconut truffles 124